Ten Steps
to Help You Write

BETTER
ESSAYS
&TERM
PAPERS

FOURTH EDITION

with comparative
MLA/APA
DOCUMENTATION

NEIL SAWERS

National Library of Canada Cataloguing
in Publication Data

Sawers, Neil,
    Ten Steps to Help You Write Better Essays
    & Term Papers – (4th Edition)

    Includes bibliographical references.
    ISBN 978-0-9697901-9-8

    1. Report writing. 2. English language--Rhetoric.
    I. Title.
PE1478.S39 2002 808'.042 C2002-910725-3

Production Credits:
4th edition: Lu Ziola
Cover and text design: Ronda Petersen
Layout: Lori St. Martin

PRINTED IN CANADA

10 9 8 7 6 5 4 3 2 1

About the 4th edition

Ten Steps started out in 1991 as an idea. I was living in Victoria, British Columbia, on Canada's West Coast. As a writer, I was looking for material on writing essays. I checked out the bookstore at the University of Victoria and found these huge books but nothing succinct and to the point. That led to the 1st edition of Ten Steps in 1993 in Toronto. The 2nd edition followed in 1995, then the 3rd edition in 2000. Some 35,000 + sales later, here is the 4th edition.

The purpose of Ten Steps is very simple; it's about communication. How can we help you write and communicate what you want to say more easily and effectively?

Why this book should be important to you

Most people think of a book on writing essays and term papers as something they'll only need in school. For me, it's a total waste of time if all you get out of this book is something to use while studying for that degree, certificate or diploma. What I want you to get out of this book are skills that will last a lifetime, whatever your career or vocation. Ten Steps contains key tools and concepts that will help you write a business proposal, a screenplay, a videogame, a report, a musical, content for your website, and a speech to shareholders. I'm not kidding. This book will help you in all those – in fact any writing you do. So please, just don't think of Ten Steps as only about academic writing, helpful as that may be.

Changes in the 4th Edition

Major changes in the 4th edition are in Step 5, Do The Research, and Step 6 on Organizing and Developing Your Outline. Both these sections have been totally reworked. As part of Step 5, we've updated the APA/MLA comparison for documenting references.

How to Use This Book

If this is your first time, I suggest you read Ten Steps right through. After that, focus on the areas that are most important to you. I will offer one piece of advice; get to know The Clarifying Steps, especially the introduction that deals with the up-front work, and Step 3, Come Up With the Right Topic. The information in these sections will always be of value to you.

In terms of format, the right-hand page provides detailed information. To help you remember this information, the left-hand page highlights key points.

Acknowledgements

I'd like to acknowledge and thank some people who made exceptional contributions to the 4th Edition. Milly Ryan-Harshman is Professor of Nursing in the Nursing Program at the University of Ontario Institute of Technology (UOIT) in Oshawa. Her contribution to Step 6 on Organizing and Developing Your Outline was invaluable. So too was the contribution of Robert Desmarais, Head, Bruce Peel Special Collections Library at the University of Alberta in Edmonton. Robert's input to the updated Step 5 on Research makes a huge difference to this section. My friend and colleague, Patrick O'Neill, President of Extraordinary Conversations in Toronto, has generously passed on his expertise on the skills involved in Listening and Speaking, also for the Research section. I received great advice from Catherine Scott, Ph.D., especially in reviewing the thesis section and from librarian Laura Scott on both research and the help librarians can give students. Finally, I love and appreciate the support I get from my wife, Marilyn Scott. Producing the 4th Edition is a mutual effort.

Permissions

If you are an instructor or student and wish to quote from this book, or show excerpts on screen, you are free to do so. I request only that you acknowledge the source.

Be proactive

(Step 1)

Plan your work

(Step 2)

THE BASIC STEPS

Two Basic Steps can help you carry out your assignments more effectively. They are:

1. **Be proactive**

   Deals with attitude and is about boldness and taking the initiative.

2. **Plan your work**

   What must you do, by when, to complete your work on time?

A brief comment on the word **proactive**. It's become a buzzword, used and more often abused, especially in business. Like relevant, authentic, meaningful, and innovative, proactive has picked up the label of gobbledygook. It's overused. So why is it still in this book? Because no other word conveys precisely what I mean. This is the go-beyond-where-you-stop attitude; taking that extra step that often feels uncomfortable, but you take it anyway. So even if you don't like or use the word, act the meaning. It will reward you.

Proactivity:

Going out of your way
to seek out and take
the initiative

*Don't let fear stop
you from trying
something new*

be proactive

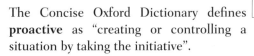

The Concise Oxford Dictionary defines **proactive** as "creating or controlling a situation by taking the initiative".

Successful people are invariably proactive whether in school, sports, music, business or any other field. In this context, being proactive means going that extra step to complete an assignment successfully. For example:

- Doing that extra research

- Calling up a newspaper editor or government expert to get a different slant on a topic

- Emailing an author or blogger for their opinion or advice

- Speaking to an instructor to clarify expectations for an assignment

If you approach every assignment proactively, it can often lead to easier completion and a better product.

Dealing with negatives and fear

Negatives are so often connected with an essay or term paper assignment. We believe it's going to be hard. Well-meaning instructors and textbooks reinforce this with comments like *"You may find this a difficult assignment,"* and *"It's not easy."*

Go for the positive *"I can do this,"* and ignore what others think. Don't let fear stop you from moving forward, whether it's fear of change, fear of doing something wrong, fear of the risk involved or simply the fear of being different.

I'm not so naïve as to suggest that things will always go smoothly. You will hit roadblocks. But if you say, *"Yes, I can,"* your chances of producing the results you want are far better.

Each step in this book is designed to help you be proactive and get the job done.

One of the first ways to *be proactive* is ...

*Good planning
will help you*

*Plan based
on the due date
of your assignment*

*How many hours
will you need?*

plan your work

Here's the picture: you've got an essay due Monday and a paper at midterm. How do you make sure that you complete both on time?

Some of us don't have a problem. We just figure it out and do it. Others leave things to the last minute, get very focused and the job gets done. This last minute stuff, however, can be stressful and you may not do your best work.

And then there's the world we live in. We're in a time crunch and thanks to e-mail, text messaging, social networks and other new technologies, we can never be clear of school, home and work. If someone wants to get hold of us, they can do so virtually immediately.

In school, at work, teachers and employers demand more results in less and less time. Essays and term papers, to do them justice, require focused effort. It's therefore more important than ever to set aside the time you need by planning for it in your schedule.

What must I do, by when, to complete this assignment on time?

Let's say you're given an assignment on November 4th to be turned in on the 12th. That's eight days. What steps should you take?

1. *Make your plan based on the date your assignment is due*

2. *Figure out how many hours it will take to carry out the assignment*

Your own experience will give you a rough idea how long it takes to do something. How much time for research and analysis? For writing and revising? Sure it may be a guesstimate, but at least it's a guide.

Due date _____

HOURS REQUIRED:	Min	Max	By When
Topic/Thesis	_____	_____	_____
Research	_____	_____	_____
Outline/Action plan	_____	_____	_____
Writing/Revision	_____	_____	_____
Contingency	_____	_____	_____
Total hours	_____	_____	_____

*Work back from the
due date to determine
your start date*

Prioritize your activities

When I estimate, I use minimum and maximum hours to give me flexibility. I also add time for contingencies (emergencies) because other factors invariably come up to complicate things. For November 12th you might need:

	MINIMUM	MAXIMUM
Topic/Thesis	1.0	1.5
Research	2.5	3.0
Outline/Action plan	2.0	3.0
Writing/Revision	7.0	8.0
Contingency	1.0	2.0
TOTAL HOURS	13.5	17.5

3. Determine your start date

Let's say you need 15 hours to carry out the assignment. How many hours can you spare per day given other school and personal priorities? For our purposes, let's assume you have up to three hours per day. To get 15 hours, you will need five days to complete the assignment. You'd have to begin by November 7th in order to hand the assignment in on the 12th.

On the other hand, if you have the time, you could cram it all into a couple of days. At least you know your options.

*Schedule the time
in your calendar*

*Stick to the
schedule or
"work your plan"*

4. Schedule the time in your calendar

However you decide to allocate your time, slot the hours the assignment requires into your calendar on a daily basis. You may have to reshuffle other activities to fit within your priorities.

5. Stick to the schedule or "work your plan"

Self discipline is the key to this. When you work your plan, you:

- Reduce pressure on yourself
- Avoid a time crunch
- Even out the work
- Build in flexibility
- Provide an opportunity for later review
- Maybe even give yourself some free time

Remember, time is precious, limited and yours. Use it well. The Clarifying Steps that follow will help you make the best use of your time.

Come up with the right topic

(Step 3)

Identify your thesis

(Step 4)

Do the research

(Step 5)

Develop the organization/outline

(Step 6)

THE CLARIFYING STEPS

There are four Clarifying Steps. They are:

- **Come up with the right topic**
- **Identify your thesis**
- **Do the research**
- **Develop the organization/outline**

The Clarifying Steps underpin the writing process. They're designed to help you get clear about:

a. The topic you're choosing
b. What you intend to prove about it, and,
c. How to carry it out.

The order of these steps is not locked in. You can just as easily be researching the topic, identifying your thesis, or organizing your ideas, all at the same time. What is important is the up-front work you carry out.

Why the up-front work is so important

If you take the time to do the up-front work before you start writing a draft, it will pay off.

Whenever I write for myself or clients, I frequently use tools like mind mapping, brainstorming and rapidwriting (freewriting).

I research the assignment to see what I can find out about it. I'll write a lot down, I'll talk to people and ask questions, I'll read, I'll explore library reference sections and databases. I'll check the Internet.

A topic I've wanted to explore is about pop music. I contend that most of today's hits won't stand the test of time. As part of my research I'd go back through a magazine/website like Billboard and see whether the top songs from the 70s, 80s and 90s are still popular today. The results would give me a guide as to what the future might hold for today's top sellers.

One way to explain the importance of doing this up-front work is with an inverted triangle, often used to demonstrate success in sales.

Normal triangle

Preparation
time

Writing
time

Scattered focus

Inverted triangle

Preparation
time

Writing
time

More focus

Normal triangle –
not enough information

Too often a salesperson tries to close a sale without uncovering the wants and needs of the customer. For example, in the auto industry, some salespeople try and fit the car to the customer. They don't spend enough time (the apex of the triangle) to determine what kind of vehicle the customer wants and why. The customer is confused, has lots of questions and objections, and it's much harder for the salesperson to close the sale. The broad base of the triangle indicates this scattered focus and direction.

Inverted triangle –
emphasizes up-front work

In the inverted triangle, the salesperson takes the time to find out exactly what the customer needs and wants. What is the customer to use this vehicle for? City or highway driving? Kids to sports practice or dance classes? Environmental concerns? Budget? Whatever the needs and wants the salesperson takes the time to uncover them. The salesperson then points out the vehicles that will fit those needs. The broad base of the inverted triangle emphasizes the value of that up-front work and points down to the apex. The result is clear focus and direction. The sale is much easier to make.

The lesson of the inverted triangle

When you do the up-front work your focus is on where you want to go. This same rule applies to writing essays and term papers. If you spend more time to get clear from the start where you're going and how to get there, doing the necessary research/analysis and obtaining key information, you'll require less time and effort for the actual writing. You're more focused and there's a huge potential payoff in that the work you do will be that much better.

Topic Criteria:

- In your study area
- Interest you
- Be of value
- Accepted by your instructor

come up with the right topic

For some people, this step is rarely a problem. For others, coming up with the right topic is challenging and creates mental blocks. Here's a pathway to help get you where you want to go.

Who selects the topic?

The topic is either:

1. Chosen after discussion between you and your instructor

2. Determined by your instructor

3. Selected by you alone

If your instructor has determined the topic, your job is to think about that topic, research it and come up with a thesis – i.e. what you want to prove about the topic.

If you get to choose the topic

When the choice of topic has been left completely or partly with you, your topic should meet four basic criteria:

* *Be in your area of study*

* *Interest you* – i.e. you're excited about it – you enjoy it

* *Be of value* – i.e. you have something valuable to communicate

* *Accepted as suitable by your instructor*

Sometimes you know exactly the topic you want to cover and your thesis regarding the topic.

Other times you're not sure, don't know, or you're blocked. We've all been there. I suggest that you literally go on an exploration to uncover that topic, using some very practical techniques along with some remarkable tools.

Do not let fear

stop you from trying

these tools & techniques

Explore to

uncover the topic

Relax and give

yourself time

to think

PRACTICAL TECHNIQUES FOR EXPLORING A TOPIC

Before we begin, a reminder about fear. In Step 1, Be Proactive, we stressed the importance of not letting fear stop you from taking action. The techniques and tools that follow are incredibly valuable. Use them to take action.

Thinking

We're usually so busy that we don't believe there's enough time to sit back and think about what we're trying to accomplish. Many successful people, however, regularly take breaks from what they're doing simply to focus their attention on new subjects, or areas that they're concerned about.

I recommend that you give yourself some quiet time to reflect. Take a walk, sit back at home, go have coffee somewhere – and let your mind flow free. Ideas have a chance to surface, patterns start to emerge, relationships begin to form.

Always carry a notebook so that you can jot your ideas down and not forget them. You can always leave a message on your cell phone, or send yourself a text message.

While you're thinking, consider your reader. What is your reader expecting? (We go into more detail in Step 7 – Write with Your Reader in Mind.)

Time to think is valuable at any stage; whether you're researching the topic, wondering what your thesis should be, or simply organizing and writing your presentation.

Explore with prewriting

Explore through research

Exploration tools

- Brainstorming
- Mind mapping
- Rapidwriting (Freewriting)

Prewriting

Prewriting is a practical way to explore. It simply means doing some exploratory writing in the topic area. Many teachers encourage this because, like thinking, it opens your mind to other possibilities. Things you write down can jell into a topic that can seem promising (or not) and uncover ideas, insights and options that you may not have considered.

How much time should you take for this up-front work? That depends on how many hours, days or weeks you have for the assignment. I suggest you build in time to prewrite – even if it's only half an hour to an hour. Increase the time based on the size and scope of the assignment.

Research

One more practical approach is through research. Research, which we'll cover more fully in Step 5, can also open up new ideas, send you off in a different direction, or confirm where you're headed. Is a topic worth pursuing? Is there enough material? Research may provide an answer.

Tools to Help You Explore

The following tools will fully support your efforts, not just in school or college, but throughout your career. They are:
- Brainstorming
- Mind mapping
- Rapidwriting (Freewriting)

These three tools make use of the random and often remarkable ways in which our minds come up with different thoughts and ideas. They allow us to get these thoughts and ideas down on paper, and in the case of mind mapping, display them in an organized manner.

Using these tools in your exploration process will help you get clear:
a. About your topic
b. What you want to prove about it, and
c. How to organize/outline it for writing.

21

Brainstorming rules:

- Write down every idea
- No censorship
- No judgment
- No evaluation
- No editing

Once the ideas are down,
evaluate each idea
then pick the topic with
the best potential

Brainstorming

Brainstorming is a freewheeling session, by yourself or with others, in which you focus on a topic or area you wish to examine more closely. In this session you let every idea about the topic come up, and, no matter how far fetched or crazy it seems, you write it down.

Start with a clear desk and a clean sheet of paper. You can also use a chalkboard, whiteboard, flip chart or computer.

If two or three of you are working together, it helps if one person acts as a recorder, making sure that everything the group thinks of gets written down.

Do's and don'ts while brainstorming

- Do write down each idea, one after the other
- Don't censor yourself
- Don't evaluate or judge anything
- Don't edit anything
- If friends or classmates assist you, don't let them censor, judge or edit either

Review the results

Once the ideas are down:

- Evaluate what you've got
- Eliminate those ideas that don't work
- Select the topic with the most potential from those that remain

Brainstorming is a great way to begin exploring options, especially when ideas are given unrestricted flow. Combining this technique with mind mapping, however, can really make a difference to your results.

Stuck in brainstorming? Focus on the other side of the topic. That may give you some clues.

Mind mapping:

- Write down main topic area in middle of page
- Create a branch for each different thought or idea
- Add ideas that pertain to existing branches to those branches
- If it's a totally new idea, create a new branch

Mind mapping *

Mind mapping is one of the most valuable tools I have ever come across, not just for writing, but for planning and exploration of all kinds.

With mind mapping:

- The topic area you're exploring is written down in the middle of a sheet of paper or chalkboard/whiteboard.

- Every thought, every idea about that topic, or area of interest from which a topic might come, goes down on the paper or chalkboard as branches on a map. (The key points that come out of your notes, your research, what you've read – all get added to the branches.) It is these branches that give order and flow to your random thoughts and ideas.

- Each branch represents similar thoughts and ideas. Any new thought or idea pertaining to an existing branch is added to that branch.

- A totally new idea, with no relation to an existing branch, receives a branch of its own.

The result is like looking at a tree from above – you see a trunk with all kinds of branches spreading from it, each with its own categories of information.

Once your thoughts, ideas, notes are down on paper, you can analyze what you've got. Which are the most important branches? What connections are there between branches? Is there a logical place from which a topic could come?

Over the next few pages you can see how these mind maps are created and evolve.

(Here are a couple of web references on mind mapping. The first is Tony Buzan's website at http://www.thinkbuzan.com. The other is Phil Chambers' Learning Technology Newsletter at http://www.learning-tech.co.uk.)

* *Clustering* and *branching* are similar techniques to mind mapping.

Conventional mind map

- Subject in middle (healthier world)
- Branches (history, food & water, education, disease prevention)

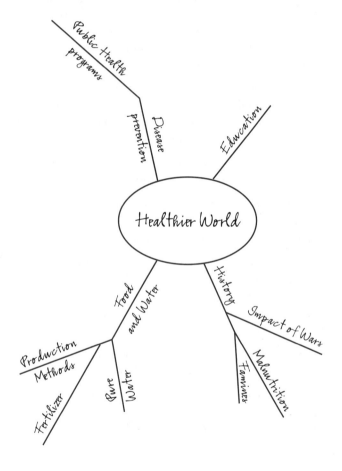

APPLICATION

I'm going to give you two practical examples. The first uses the mind map approach we've just covered. The second is a unique way of using sticky notes.

Conventional mind map approach

Let's assume that as part of a sociology program you have to write something about the improved health of the world compared to a century ago. The topic is in that area but you're unsure what it will be. Here's how to begin using the mind map process:

Take a clean sheet of paper, or chalkboard and in the middle, write down the area you want to explore. In this case write healthier world.

Immediately your mind starts to conjure up thoughts about health in its many permutations. Because it's such a large subject, you decide to focus on health in the developing world.

What health problems did countries in the developing world face? That historical perspective is your first branch. Some of the sub-topics that you might come up with include malnutrition, tropical diseases, childhood diseases, and dysentery.

With your pen or chalk, you place this first branch off the central core. Now you brainstorm other areas which may require new branches, or additions to branches you've already created.

- There's a *disease prevention* branch – every thought or idea about how diseases were prevented over the last 100 years goes down here; vaccines, better professional care, purifying the water, controlling sewage. These measures helped lessen death and disease, creating a healthier population where more children survive and older people live longer.

Mind Map (Complete)

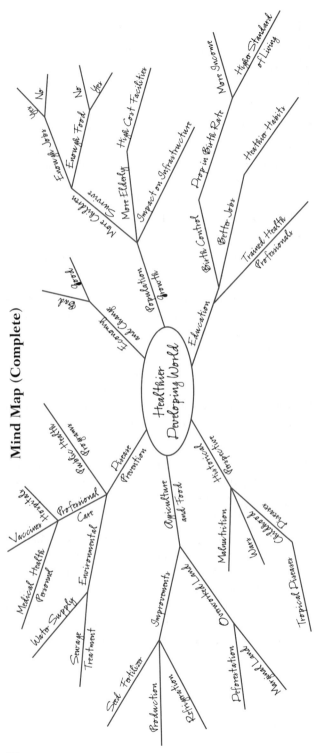

- You recognize that *education* plays a major role – so that's a new branch. Included in that branch are public health programs, the training of medical professionals and other health workers, such as environmental health.

- There's an *agriculture & food* branch. The last 100 years have seen dramatic improvements in agriculture and food production. There's better seed, fertilizers and production methods creating more food. On the other hand there's land not able to support a growing population because of poor quality soils, flooding, lack of water, and erosion from deforestation.

- There's a *population* branch. More children are alive because of vaccines, better hygiene, and better food and water. On the other hand, lower death rates have increased the population. In some countries the food supply can't keep up, leading to malnutrition, starvation and death.

- There's an *economy* branch. How has the increased population affected the economy? Are there more jobs? Are jobs scarce? Has it been a drain on national resources?

As you let your mind wander, you'll find that your ideas come from many different places. Add those ideas to the branches you've created. If it's a totally new idea, create another branch.

Using sticky notes

Disease prevention

Historical perspective

Vaccination

Malnutrition

Sewage systems

Impact of wars

Maternal Health Programs

Childhood Diseases

Sticky notes mind map approach

From the previous example each key point is written on a sticky note. We then put it on a surface like a flip chart or wall. Flip charts work well because the size of the paper gives plenty of space.

Now, instead of branches you create columns to represent each branch:

- At the top of the column, place a general heading of what that column is about

- Every sticky note pertaining to that column goes underneath it

- Create a new column if it's a different area altogether

- Use as many columns as there are branches

On the following double page, you can see what happens when using sticky notes.

Using Sticky Notes (Complete)

Healthier Developing World

- State of Economy
  - Resources
  - Population Skills
- Population Growth
  - More Children Survive
  - More Elderly
- Education
  - General
    - Better Jobs
  - Health
    - Trained Health Personnel
- Disease Prevention
  - Public and Environmental Health
    - Water and Sewage Treatment
  - Professional Care
    - Medical Health Professionals
- Historical Perspective
  - Limited Life Span
  - Malnutrition
- Agriculture and Food
  - Overworked Land
    - Deforestation
      - erosion
      - flooding
  - Improvements
    - Seed Fertilizer

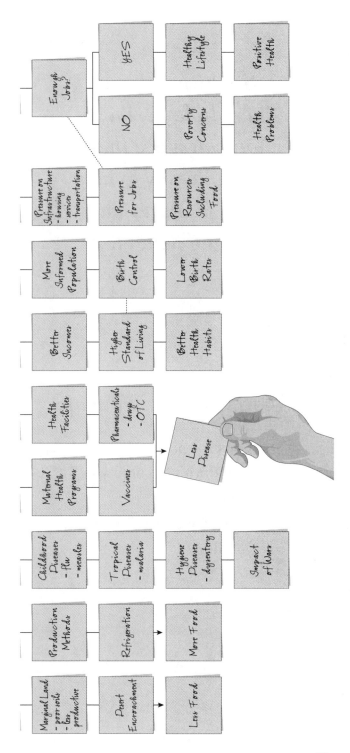

33

Sticky notes have incredible flexibility. You can move them around easily to help you plan, review, create flow, etc.

Analyze your mind map:

- Look for patterns
- What bridges could you create?
- What conclusions could you draw?

Here's the magic of using sticky notes. Because of the unique quality of the product, you can:

- Move a sticky note around

- If something doesn't fit in one column and belongs in another, you can move it there

- Move items around in an individual column until you're satisfied that the items are in a sequence you can work with

Conventional mind map system or sticky notes?

For me, the connections are more visible on the conventional system, especially when I'm dealing with only a few branches. If you have a lot of branches, with many sub headings, sticky notes may be more manageable.

Mind map analysis

Once the information is down, analyze what you've got. Look for patterns. How does one branch (or column if you use sticky notes) relate to another? What bridges could you create? What other connections are there? What conclusions could you draw?

In my experience, when you create a mind map, the important things jump out at you. You start to see how and where all your thoughts, ideas and research connect together. A direction for the topic, and what you want to prove about it, shows up.

This helps determine the sequence of your essay or term paper, and often gives you ideas and connections, even conclusions, you might not have considered.

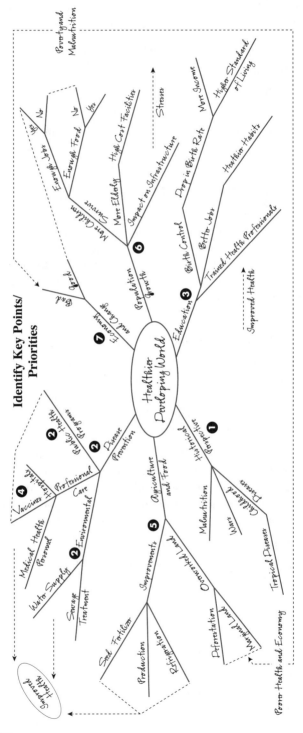

Identify Key Points/ Priorities

Healthier Developing World

Poverty and Malnutrition

7 Economy and Living
Good
Bad

6 Population Growth
More Children Survive
Enough Food — No — Yes
High Cost Facilities
More Elderly
Impact on Infrastructure
Stresses

3 Education
Birth Control
Drop in Birth Rate
More Income
Higher Standard of Living
Better Jobs
Healthier Habits
Trained Health Professionals
Improved Health

1 Historical Perspective
Malnutrition
War
Childhood Diseases
Tropical Diseases
Poorer Health and Economy

5 Agriculture and Food
Overpopulation and Management
Deforestation
Improvements
Seed Fertilizer
Production
Refrigeration

2 Disease Prevention
2 Public Health Programs
2 Environmental
Water Supply
Sewage Treatment
Medical Health Personnel
4 Hospitals
Professional Care
Vaccines

Improving Health

You may also see where too much emphasis has been applied in one area and too little in another. If one area looks thin, you might need more research, or, question whether to go down a particular path.

Identify key points and/or priorities

Next, identify the key points, or priorities. In which sequence should they be discussed? By numbering them you give yourself the natural, step by step, linear sequence to work with when developing your outline.

Here's how that might work using the health care example. If you look at the mind map on the opposite page, you will see that I have numbered certain areas. To me, they are the key points or priorities with which to deal. I see historical perspectives as the first priority, followed by disease prevention – notably basic areas like public health programs and environmental concerns, such as water supply and treatment of sewage.

If we assume that our topic is "The impact of health care in the developing world over the last 100 years", here are the key points in sequence, as identified on the mind map:

1. Historical health problems

2. Importance of disease prevention in improving health, specifically public health & environmental programs

3. Public education – in both health and general terms and its benefits

4. Health care resources – people, facilities, programs

5. Improved agriculture/food production

6. Impact of population growth – stress on infrastructure, land, transportation, etc.

7. Impact of changes on the economy

You can now use this seven point sequence as an outline for developing or organizing your material in preparation for writing your first draft.

Try **rapidwriting** *to uncover fresh thoughts and ideas about your topic…it only takes a few minutes*

Rapidwriting rules:

- Write nonstop
- No censoring
- No correcting
- No judgment

Review what you wrote:

- Highlight key points to add to your mind map/organizing

Rapidwriting (Freewriting)

I'd like to introduce you to one more tool. It's called rapidwriting (or freewriting) and it can be very useful in giving you fresh ideas about your topic.

Although similar to brainstorming, with rapidwriting you let the mind flow with the topic, doing anything it wants, writing down insights, making comparisons – all without limitation. Nothing is taboo. You can make judgments and evaluations; you can express your views in the moment.

In rapidwriting you write, nonstop, for a fixed period of time. Here are the rules:

• Give yourself a time frame – it might be five minutes, 15 minutes, half an hour – to write about your topic. (Some believe you can only focus for a few minutes. I find that I can go 15 minutes or more when I hit my stride. Whatever works for you is fine.)

• Don't stop – just let the words and ideas flow

• Don't censor yourself

• Don't decide if what you've written is good or bad

• Don't change anything, don't correct, don't say, "I shouldn't have written that!"

When the time is up, examine what you've written. I am amazed at the wealth of information that can be generated from this simple exercise. Underline or highlight the key points, or whatever you consider of value, and add this new information to your mind map, or however you organize your work.

Summary

These techniques – brainstorming, mind mapping, rapid-writing – can be used at any time for many different purposes. They are extremely valuable in helping you get clear about where you're going.

Is your topic viable?

- Check it
- Test it
- Will it fly?
- Are there holes big enough to drive a truck through?

IS THE TOPIC VIABLE?

Before you finalize your topic, make sure it's viable. In business they test something by making a prototype or giving a new service a trial run prior to committing full resources to a project. An example from the aircraft industry is the chicken test. When aircraft take off or land, birds are sometimes sucked into the intakes of jet engines. Manufacturers have to be certain that an engine will keep running if birds are a problem. So, they fire dead chickens into the intake of an engine prototype. If the engine continues to perform satisfactorily, the project continues.

Another wonderful phrase I heard for reviewing a film script could also apply: Are there holes big enough in your topic to drive a truck through?

What test will you apply to your topic to determine if it's viable?

Is what I'm working on good enough to fly? Can I drive a truck through it? Do I have enough research to back up my opinions or to challenge them? Can I develop this topic in enough depth or am I wasting my time? By discovering any shortcomings early, you save time and effort. Then you can start looking for a fresh angle to your topic, or a new topic entirely.

*Consider limiting
(or expanding) your
topic so as to better focus
on a specific area*

*How might you
narrow down and define
your topic effectively?*

LIMITING (OR EXPANDING) THE TOPIC

You could write a book on some topics. On the other hand, you may find that you have to expand the topic for your discussion to be of value.

I'm going to concentrate on the need to limit a topic – a topic that might otherwise cover too much ground. By determining limits, you narrow the focus. This lets you fully explore and develop a specific area.

For example, when we discussed mind mapping we suggested a topic for sociology about the improved health of the world today compared to a century ago. Since it was such a broad topic, we narrowed it down to "health in the developing world".

Even that's a very broad topic. We could narrow it down even more by considering only the health of children in the developing world.

We could further limit the topic by discussing the impact of vaccination programs on these children.

You can also narrow down an assignment. Suppose your English essay was "Hamlet: insane or just faking it?" The focused version might be "What does Hamlet's relationship with Ophelia tell us of the central character and his state of mind?"

In summary, the reason for narrowing or limiting a topic is because the scope is usually too broad to allow the desired detailed analysis and discussion.

*If a topic won't fit,
don't try to force it*

*Do you know what
your instructor expects
from you?*

Assume nothing

*Be proactive and
find out*

Caution! Too often students believe a topic has to look a particular way even if it doesn't feel right. As a result, many students get locked into a position where they try and force things to fit that simply don't.

Avoid this situation. If it feels wrong, find another topic. Or, if you still feel what you've chosen does have possibilities, then make sure you have facts and research to support what you're doing.

WHAT DOES MY INSTRUCTOR EXPECT FROM ME?

Students often complain that they get an assignment from their instructor but are not told what the instructor expects from them. This usually shows up after an assignment is done with instructor comments like, "This is not what the assignment was about." Or, "Why didn't you do this?"

Two things could be going on here. Either you misunderstood what the instructor was after, or, the instructor did not clarify what was wanted from the assignment.

How can you prevent this? The worst thing is to make assumptions about what you think your instructor intends. We all know the problems caused by wrong assumptions.

The answer is *be proactive*. If you're not certain what your instructor expects, ask. The best instructors encourage it.

A thesis tells your reader what you will argue in your paper.

Your argument is based on:

- Evidence you have gathered
- Research that points to a particular conclusion

Your success is a result of:

- Having a clear, forceful and supportable argument
- The ability to persuade your reader of the validity of that argument

identify your thesis

Your thesis is the key element upon which your essay or term paper is grounded. Without a solid, supportable thesis, the reader will question the work's validity.

So, *what is a thesis?*

DEFINITION

A thesis is a guide for your reader. It tells your reader what you will argue in your paper. This argument is based on:

- Evidence you have gathered
- Research that points to a particular conclusion

Success is a result of:

1. Having a clear, forceful and supportable argument
2. Being able to persuade your reader of the validity of that argument.

The question to ask yourself, is therefore "Do I have a sound argument, backed by solid research and supported by evidence, that I can present to my reader?"

Let me give you a couple of examples. The first is from Shakespeare's Hamlet. One of the critical debates has always revolved around Hamlet's sanity. Here's the thesis:

While Hamlet is tragically indecisive, my analysis shows that he is sane. In my essay, I will explore Hamlet's initial encounter with his father's ghost, and his mistreatment of Ophelia. I will argue, based on my interpretation of these examples, that there is adequate evidence in the text to prove my claim that Hamlet is sane.

The case must be argued on the basis of the evidence in the text – not on your feelings about, in this case, the play. The reader asks, "Show me the evidence to support your argument."

The second example comes from a more modern context. With the mapping of the human genome, companies have applied for thousands of gene patents. My thesis

Keep your thesis statement handy — where you can see it or find it — so you always remember your focus

If you are unable to prove your thesis, revise it, or reconsider it

is that *patenting genes severely restricts basic research by universities and other public research institutions.* I will argue that complex patent and licensing arrangements, now in place, prevent desirable research from being undertaken today and in the future.

My job is now to persuade you that a strong case exists for not accepting patents on genes.

Tips

We suggest that in your drafts (not your final copy) you keep emphasizing and reminding yourself of your thesis by underlining it in your introduction. If you cannot identify your thesis clearly, it is doubtful whether your reader will be able to do so either.

As well, consider writing your thesis in big letters and putting it where you can see it. Take a copy in your binder when you're researching or writing, so you remember to stay on track.

Staying focused

Return to the thesis after writing each section to ensure that you are still on track. And, continue to argue your main point rather than drifting off on some tangent.

Keep asking yourself as you do additional research, "Is what I'm doing useful to my thesis?" If it isn't, either drop that point, or check to see if the thesis itself is valid.

Can you revise your thesis?

You do not have to stick to a thesis that cannot be proven. What if you find that as you go through various drafts, the evidence doesn't materialize, or draws you to a different conclusion? If this is the case, revise your thesis or reconsider it.

Summary

Your argument needs to be based on solid, factual support. Your empirical evidence can be a text, a report, a study, an article – but keep in mind that this evidence must persuade the reader to accept the validity of your position.

Research helps you to uncover your topic and provide evidence to support (or counter) your thesis

Be thorough in your research

Avoid handing in assignments that are:
- Thin on ideas and concepts
- Full of padding

Upside of technology

- Major advances in ability to do research
- Huge increases in the amount and scope of information available

Downside of technology

- Many students don't realize that the best sources for research are the large specialty databases, not Google or other search engines

do the research

5

There are three elements to this section on research:

1. The Research Process itself
2. A special section on Listening and Speaking, especially helpful for interviews, discussing your needs with people, such as librarians, and for asking questions.
3. Documentation – how to document the sources you use.

THE RESEARCH PROCESS

Research is carried out in order to find pertinent information about your topic so that you have solid material to support your ideas and arguments. What have others said about your topic? What new data exists? How will it support your point of view? Or will it? Don't be surprised if what you find makes you shift the emphasis of your topic or thesis in some way.

Have I done enough research?

Instructors often complain that students don't take their research far enough. They base that opinion on assignments that are thin or skimpy on ideas and concepts, and full of padding. Your objective is to make sure that in addition to your own thinking, class notes and textbooks, you do sufficient research for your assignment to be as thorough as possible.

GENERAL RESEARCH INFORMATION

Since this book was first published in 1993, technology has delivered major advances in the ability to do research. It has also resulted in huge increases in the amount and scope of information available.

The technology has a downside. Many students with their cell phones, iPads, e-mail and Internet search knowhow, don't realize or appreciate that the best sources of information for academic purposes are not on Google or other search engines, but on large specialty databases. These databases are costly to develop, maintain and access, which is why only university and college libraries, government libraries, and libraries of major organizations can afford them. These databases contain a wealth of information unavailable anywhere else.

Your student card usually gives you free access to
specialty databases.

*Remember the
importance of diversity.
Information comes from
a wide variety of sources*

*In research there are
<u>primary</u> and <u>secondary</u>
sources to go to for
information. Use the
primary sources first*

What is a Primary Source?

- An original source document or physical object
- Written or created during the time under study

The good news for students. Your college student card usually gives you access to your library's databases at no charge – it's part of your tuition fee. Even if you're not a student, you can probably get a temporary card from the library to use these databases, either for free or at a reasonable cost.

I'm not saying that you shouldn't use search engines like Google and Bing. But use caution. I'll have more to say about that later.

The importance of search diversity

Information is not found in one place. It comes from a variety of sources, both primary and secondary. I suggest that you carry out research in many different areas. In that way you give yourself the most diversified information for your project, sometimes from unexpected but useful sources.

PRIMARY AND SECONDARY SOURCES

Research information is derived from both primary and secondary sources. Defining these can be an issue for some students so we'll try and clear up any confusion. Let me stress one point here. When it comes to research, use the primary sources first.

What is a primary source?

A primary source is an originating source document or physical object. It was written or created during the time under study by someone or some organization directly involved in the event. The source offers an inside view of that event. Primary sources include:

Original Documents such as manuscripts, letters, diaries, speeches, interviews, news videos, official records

Creative Works such as plays, poems, novels, paintings, songs, photographs

Relics or Artifacts such as pottery, tools, furniture, clothing, buildings

What is a Secondary Source?

- A published or unpublished document at least one step removed from primary sources
- May describe, interpret, analyze or be based on primary sources

Where to look for sources

Library reference sections
- Encyclopedias, bibliographies, catalogs
- Helpful, professional librarians

Here are some examples of primary sources:
- Sir John Franklin's diary – Attempts to find the Northwest Passage in the early 1800's
- A Rembrandt painting
- A journal article reporting breakthroughs in medical or scientific research
- News footage of the 2011 Japanese earthquake and tsunami
- Survivor interviews from the 2010 Haitian earthquake
- Dinosaur fossils from the Alberta badlands – Royal Tyrell Museum, Drumheller
- First folio of Shakespeare's plays
- Congressional Record – the official record of the proceedings and debates of the United States Congress

What is a secondary source?

A secondary source is something that is published or unpublished that is at least one step removed from the primary source. This source may describe, interpret, analyze or be based on primary sources. Secondary sources include journal articles, textbooks, biographies, encyclopedias.

Here are some examples of secondary sources:
- A journal article that critiques a Shakespeare play
- A biography of Eleanor Roosevelt
- Encyclopedia Britannica, Wikipedia
- A book about the impact of The Beatles on 20th century pop music

WHERE TO LOOK FOR SOURCES

You're ready to start your research. Here are some places to look:

Library reference sections

I love library reference sections. They contain so many useful resources such as encyclopedias, bibliographies and unique catalogues. Their best resources, however, are the reference librarians themselves who just happen to be some of the most informed and helpful people around. They can point you in the right direction. They can tell you how to use the various indexes and catalogues available. They'll help focus searches for you. They'll clue you in on the online databases that are often so critical in finding what you're looking for. *Use them.*

Where to look for sources (cont.)

Books
- Your textbooks
- Other appropriate texts

Online databases
- Specialty discipline
- Very sophisticated
- Easy to search
- Credible articles
- Peer reviewed (refereed)

Caution:

Most articles on the Internet, however good they are or appear to be, are not subjected to peer review

University and public libraries are not the only places with reference sections. Material may also be available from corporations, governments, museums, newspapers and archives.

Books

Your required course texts are major sources of information. The bibliographies in those texts may guide you to other useful material. You can also search under the topic and see what other books are available.

Online Databases

The most current thinking and research on a particular subject, discipline or activity is usually found in the articles published in that discipline, either in online or printed journals. Articles that appear in a specific discipline's database tend to have greater credibility as being authentic, accurate and reliable. Peer review is why.

Peer review

Articles in specialty journals are perceived to have more validity because they are almost always peer reviewed (or refereed), indicating that the author's work has met the standards required for publication in that discipline.

The vast majority of articles in article directories on the Internet don't go through peer review. This isn't to say that an article doesn't have good information. It may in fact be first rate. Its authenticity just hasn't been judged by peers. If you decide to add such an article as a reference in an essay or term paper you need to qualify this fact.

Other databases

Many other databases are available for access, including those of major newspapers such as The New York Times and The Globe & Mail. Access to newspapers, periodicals and magazines around the world are available on the Internet. If using these resources for information on your topic and they're not peer reviewed, try to find other sources to support your findings.

George Boole was a working class kid born in Lincoln in England in 1815, the year Napoleon was defeated at Waterloo. George was a mathematical genius, much of it self-taught. He came up with a type of linguistic algebra, based on a binary approach, processing only two objects – the "yes-no", "true-false", "on-off", "one zero". His work is regarded as critical to the development of the modern computer. I doubt if George Boole ever thought he'd make it into the history books of the 21st century.

Sources: *Encyclopaedia Brittanica*, *Wikipedia* and *Kerry Redshaw* (www.kerryR.net)

Boolean Search

- Select keywords
- Limit your search using AND
  e.g. Shakespeare AND London
  or Shakespeare + London
- Broaden your search using OR
  e.g. London OR Paris OR Madrid
- Eliminate reference to a keyword using NOT
  e.g. Shakespeare AND London NOT Stratford
  or Shakespeare + London –Stratford

NB: Use CAPS for Boolean operators AND OR NOT.

When using the minus sign for NOT, place it immediately before the affected keyword and precede it with a space. See Bullet 4 above.

An activity you might want to pursue is to check the latest journals in your areas of interest. I browse current journals for areas that interest me. It's amazing how often I find something I can use. Like playing a hunch, you develop a gut feel of where to look.

How to search the databases
Knowing how to search effectively is a skill that will always be of value to you. And you'd better thank George Boole because in coming up with what we call a Boolean search, George Boole made the job a whole lot easier.

What a Boolean search does is help you search in the best possible way, narrowing down the area you need to search, or expanding it, or removing words that can confuse or complicate what you're after, or permitting various search combinations in parentheses/brackets.

How to do a Boolean search
You start with the keywords you are searching for. Once you decide what they are, you can search in a number of ways using the Boolean operators AND, OR, NOT and parentheses:

1. Use AND (or +) to limit your search. The more keywords you enter connected by AND, the narrower the search. e.g. If you want to know about Shakespeare's time in London, then you'd type in the keywords <u>Shakespeare</u> and <u>London</u> as follows: Shakespeare AND London or Shakespeare + London

2. Use OR to broaden your search. The more keywords you enter connected by OR, the greater the response. e.g. If you wanted information on great European cities, your request might be: London OR Paris OR Madrid

3. Use NOT (or in some cases AND NOT or ANDNOT) to eliminate any reference to a keyword. e.g. Suppose you wanted to make sure that any reference to Stratford was eliminated from your Shakespearean search, here's what you'd do: Shakespeare AND London NOT Stratford or Shakespeare + London –Stratford

59

Boolean Search (cont.)

Use parentheses/brackets to combine more than one Boolean operator in the sequence you want; e.g. Shakespeare AND (London OR Stratford)

Individual Search

- You search an individual database

Federated Search

- You search a database that accesses several databases at once; e.g., EBSCO

Play with keywords

- Use synonyms and/or short phrases to provide search alternatives

4. Use of parentheses/brackets

When you've got more than one Boolean operator involved, you can use parentheses to combine and search for the things you want. The computer recognizes that items in parentheses are always searched first. For example, suppose you wanted more information about Shakespeare's life in both London and Stratford. Here's what you'd do:

Shakespeare AND (London OR Stratford). You'd retrieve information for Shakespeare, separately for London and Stratford, without blending them together.

Likewise you could take several keywords, such as (piano OR guitar) AND (electric OR acoustic) and come up with specific search information on these topics.

Once the search results are available, read the online abstract and see if the article content interests you.

Individual and Federated Search
You'd like to get as much information as you can from the databases. A couple of options are available to you. You can search an individual database that gives you information only from that database. You can search a federated database (for example EBSCO) that searches several combined databases. This gives you potential topic information from many other sources.

Play with the keywords
Sometimes the keywords you use in your search don't provide as much information as you'd like. If that happens, substitute synonyms or even two- or three-word phrases and try those for your search.

PEOPLE

People are often one
of your best sources
for information:

- Talk to librarians
- Consult instructors/professors
  on campus or elsewhere
- Call an expert

PEOPLE

People can be one of your best sources for information. Using them well is a proactive step.

Librarians

As I mentioned earlier, in my experience librarians are invariably helpful and valuable. Not only can they assist you to find information more quickly, but more of it – from sources you probably never thought of, or had any idea existed.

Instructors/professors

Don't be afraid to ask your instructor/professor, or other instructors/professors on campus or elsewhere, who might point you in a direction, or give you advice to further your search.

Experts

Go to experts in the area you're writing about. If you're doing a piece on documentary film, talk to a local producer or director. If you're writing about an environmental issue, speak to someone in an environmental organization – or a company representative responsible for environmental issues. If you're writing about political or economic situations, consider speaking with a newspaper editor or reporter, or, depending on where you live, your local, regional or national politicians.

I find that people are almost always willing to help. Yes, sometimes they are too busy to talk; more likely, they simply haven't been asked. In my experience it almost always pays off. After all, they can only say no.

When using the Internet, make sure that you:

- Focus on the information you need
- Obtain credible information
- Don't get sidetracked by interesting but unrelated websites
- Give yourself a time limit

Evaluating the information:

Apply The CRAAP Test

USING INTERNET SEARCH ENGINES

I admit that in doing research it's very tempting to go directly to Google and other search engines to find information. There's nothing wrong with doing this. You may get well get some good ideas. But don't make these search engines your main avenue of research. They certainly won't carry the immense amount of specialized material available in the online databases.

Besides, in using the search engines you can get sidetracked by got-to-have information, or connecting with friends on social networks. Bookmark an interesting site to check later, but not on your work schedule. Concentrate only on the research that applies to your topic.

If you plan to use a website as a research reference, evaluate that website carefully. What are the credentials of the person(s) who set up the site? How often is it updated? Is the information neutral or have a built-in bias? Based on these questions, what better time to introduce you to the CRAAP test.

Evaluating information – Applying the CRAAP Test

I'm very grateful to the Meriam Library at California State University in Chico for allowing me to use this useful handout (see next two pages). It's self-explanatory and I suggest that you pay close attention to the advice.

THE CRAA

When you search for information, you're going to find lots of it ... but is it accurate and reliable? You will have to determine this for yourself, and the CRAAP Test can help. The CRAAP Test is a list of questions to determine if the information you have is reliable. Please keep in mind that the following list is not static or complete. Different criteria will be more or less important depending on your situation or need. So, what are you waiting for? Is your web site credible and useful, or is it a bunch of . . .?!

EVALUATION CRITERIA

Currency: *The timeliness of the information.*

- When was the information published or posted?
- Has the information been revised or updated?
- Is the information current or out-of date for your topic?
- Are the links functional?

Relevance: *The importance of the information for your needs.*

- Does the information relate to your topic or answer your question?
- Who is the intended audience?
- Is the information at an appropriate level (i.e. not too elementary or advanced for your needs)?
- Have you looked at a variety of sources before determining this is one you will use?
- Would you be comfortable using this source for a research paper?

Used by kind permission of the Meriam Library, California State University, Chico, CA.

TEST

Authority: *The source of the information.*

- Who is the author/publisher/source/sponsor?
- Are the author's credentials or organizational affiliations given?
- What are the author's credentials or organizational affiliations given?
- What are the author's qualifications to write on the topic?
- Is there contact information, such as a publisher or e-mail address?
- Does the URL reveal anything about the author or source? examples: .com .edu .gov .org .net

Accuracy: *The reliability, truthfulness, and correctness of the informational content.*

- Where does the information come from?
- Is the information supported by evidence?
- Has the information been reviewed or refereed?
- Can you verify any of the information in another source or from personal knowledge?
- Does the language or tone seem unbiased and free of emotion?
- Are there spelling, grammar, or other typographical errors?

Purpose: *The reason the information exists.*

- What is the purpose of the information? to inform? teach? sell? entertain? persuade?
- Do the authors/sponsors make their intentions or purpose clear?
- Is the information fact? opinion? propaganda?
- Does the point of view appear objective and impartial?
- Are there political, ideological, cultural, religious, institutional, or personal biases?

Print a copy of Internet/Email material

Web sites are constantly changing. We recommend that you take a print copy of any source material (Internet/Email) that you plan to use in your assignment. Then, if anyone asks, you can produce it.

Record your information carefully:

- For verification
- For documentation

Never plagiarize by passing off someone else's work as your own

Keep a print copy of Internet/Email material

I recommend that you print out a copy of anything from the Internet (or Email) that you plan to use as a source, so that you can show it to someone if asked. The very nature of the web is one of change. Organizations or individuals with web sites are expected to constantly update them, provide relevant information and delete dated material. As well, the site itself may no longer exist.

A reference on its own, therefore, may not be the same, or even available. Emails also get deleted, or changed. A print copy is at least some proof.

Record information/credit your sources

Take careful notes on where you found or received your information. It's all going to be important:

- If somebody asks you where it came from so they can check it

- To go down in your list of references, or works cited. There's nothing worse than quoting something then being unable to recall where you found it, or who said it.

A note on plagiarism

Plagiarism is taking someone else's writing, music, artwork, and passing it off as your own. There have been a number of court cases in recent years where the composer of a song has been accused of stealing the tune, or the lyric, from someone else. Some of the songs were hits so the amount of money involved was substantial.

More in keeping with what we're dealing with here, I know of a student who submitted a movie review as part of a class assignment. Well aware of the student's writing style, the teacher suspected something was wrong and checked on the web. Sure enough, the student had downloaded a review from a web site. Confronted, the student admitted what he'd done. It's an important lesson. *Plagiarism leads to a failed grade.*

Some tips to

improve your

listening

and speaking

With listening, we often
fail to give the speaker
our full attention.
That's because of the
way we listen:

**"We're either speaking
or waiting to speak"**

LISTENING & SPEAKING

Good listening and speaking skills will help you get the most out of working with library staff, doing interviews, and asking questions. They also help clarify the direction you're taking with your work.

Listening

How we listen makes a difference as to whether we receive and understand what someone else is trying to tell us. How many times have you been told "You didn't hear what I said?" Or "That's not what I meant." This happens because all too often we don't give the speaker our full attention. We get distracted. The problem is the way most of us listen:

"We're either speaking or waiting to speak."

Let me explain. When we listen to someone discuss something, especially if we disagree or want to make a point about what they're saying, we stop listening. Instead, we focus on what we want to say ... we're waiting to speak. As often as not we'll interrupt the speaker with our point of view. We certainly won't catch the rest of what they have to say.

My point? If you're interviewing someone, if you're asking help from a librarian, listen to everything the other person has to say. If their viewpoint differs from yours, don't jump in to contradict it. Be curious instead. Explore the other person's perspective before you judge it. That way you'll hear and appreciate their overall point of view.

*Assumptions can
spell trouble:*

*"Did you really hear what
you thought you heard?"*

Check to find out

*With speaking,
make sure that you are:*

- Clear on what you're after
- Proactive in achieving it

Beware – assumptions can spell trouble

A journalist interviews a well known public figure. After the interview is published, the individual complains to the editor about what was written. "That's not what I said. That's not what I meant. It's been taken out of context."

Did you hear what you thought you heard?

Too often we assume something means one thing, when in fact it means another. Or we jump to a conclusion without checking it out. What's the answer? Check your assumptions. If you interview people – reporters, business people, civic officials, social advocates, whoever – listen to what they have to say, then summarize what you think you heard. They'll tell you if you're accurate or not.

Speaking

When you speak, your intention is to communicate something to another person so that they understand what you have said, and if necessary, respond. In terms of speaking with librarians, or interviewing people, two elements will be helpful to you:

- Be clear about what you want

- Be proactive

Be clear about what you want

Know what it is you're after. It's useful to prepare yourself by creating an agenda with a series of questions for which you need answers. At the same time, be prepared to explain what it is you're doing and what you hope to achieve. That gives people a better idea of what you're after and how best to help you.

*Be proactive in
contacting those who can
make a difference, or
contribution, to your
knowledge and efforts*

Document your sources

- To acknowledge the
  source
- To register where the
  source may be located

Be proactive

Many people miss out on obtaining valuable information because they're scared to contact someone or some organization. I appreciate that this can be intimidating. The proactive step, however, is to make the call. In my experience the results are invariably positive. People like to be asked for help and advice.

Summary

Listening and speaking are skills that make a difference in your ability to communicate and receive communication from others. Improving and applying these skills will absolutely help you in your research. It will also contribute in every area of life.

DOCUMENTATION

Documenting your sources is an essential element of writing essays, term papers and many other kinds of reports and submissions. There are two reasons for documentation:

1. To acknowledge the source – i.e. give credit to an author, an organization, etc.

2. To register where the source was located – whether a book, a periodical, an interview, the Internet, etc., so that if someone wishes to verify that source, they know where to find it

Giving credit to the source is pretty basic. Including the source in a list of references is more complex. It's not made easier by having several different systems, such as MLA, APA, Chicago, etc., each with its own distinctive style. What is important is that you be consistent in the system you use.

Choose the appropriate documentation style and apply it consistently

NOTE: If documenting your sources is confusing to you, you're not alone. In addition to the MLA and APA's own manuals and websites, many universities and colleges put out their own versions of these documentation styles to help their students. As well, the accuracy of software documentation systems is questionable. Our intention in the pages that follow is to provide a comparison between MLA and APA styles in the most frequently used areas. We hope it helps.

In this book we'll compare the two styles in most common use – MLA (Modern Language Association) and APA (American Psychological Association), and we'll deal only with the list of references at the end of your essay or term paper. These references are both print and electronic. In MLA style the list is called "Works Cited"; in APA style it is called "References."

Both MLA and APA require that all references:

- Are double spaced (To save space in this book, all examples are single spaced.)

- Use a hanging indent; i.e. the first line of a reference is flush left with subsequent lines indented.

Which style should you use?

Generally speaking, MLA style is used in English and the humanities. APA style is used in the social sciences. If in doubt, ask your instructor.

Updates

It's said that in life, two things are certain; death and taxes. To that you might add changes in how APA and MLA handle references. With the huge increase in electronic sources over the last decade, both APA and MLA have introduced changes to their respective systems. This will likely continue, so check APA and MLA web sites for more information, updates and answers to your questions. As well, many schools issue their own guidelines for APA and MLA, sometimes clarifying and at others confusing the process. One excellent source is Diana Hacker's website at http://bcs.bedfordstmartins.com/resdoc5e/RES5e_ch09_s1-0002.html for APA and http://bcs.bedfordstmartins.com/resdoc5e/RES5e_ch08_s1-0011.html for MLA.

MLA

General Rules

With the author, MLA lists the last name and first name as follows:

Johnston, Heather.
[Use initials if first name not known]

With the title, MLA capitalizes the first letter of major words and proper nouns.

For books and major works – italicize the title:
A Thousand Splendid Suns
For periodicals and short works – put in quotation marks:
"Jurassic Park Syndrome"

With the date:
- The date goes immediately prior to the provenance
- May, June and July are spelled in full. Abbreviate all others; e.g., Dec. Sept.
- The date sequence is day month year with no commas: 1 Jan. 2011
- If no date available, write n.d.

With the place of publication, unless the city is well known – e.g. Montreal – add the state or province (abbreviated – ON, TX, BC, NY), or name of the country.

With the provenance
- MLA wants the reader to know the medium from which the source originates; i.e., Print, Web, CD, DVD, Film, Performance, Television, Lecture, EBook.
- The provenance goes at the end of the reference.
- If the provenance is the web, the retrieval date should follow; e.g., Web. 19 Jan. 2011.

If references overlap a line, indent each additional line by 5 spaces or 1/2 inch.

Books

Last name, first name of author.
Title.
Place of publication: publisher, year of publication. Provenance.

Friedman, Thomas L. *Hot, Flat, and Crowded.*
    New York: Farrar, Strauss and Giroux, 2008. Print.

APA

General Rules

With the author, APA lists the last name followed by initial(s).

Johnston, H. L.

With the title, APA capitalizes only the first letter of the first word, proper nouns and the first word after a colon. Book titles are italicized. Titles of periodicals, newspapers and journals are not

A thousand splendid suns

With the date:
- APA always places the date of publication second, in parentheses after the author's name.
- Months are spelled in full - i.e. April, December
- The date sequence is generally year, month day:
- 2011, January 1
- If no date is available, write: (n.d.).

With the place of publication, list the name of the city, plus state or province (abbreviated – ON, TX, BC, NY), or name of the country; e.g., New York, NY:

If references overlap a line, indent each additional line by 5 spaces or 1/2 inch.

Books

Last name, initial(s) of author.
(Year of publication).
Title.
Place of publication: publisher.

Friedman, T.L. (2008). *Hot, flat, and crowded*.
    New York, NY: Farrar, Strauss and Giroux.

MLA

More than one author:
- For first author: Name, first name,
- For additional authors: first name last name, (normally use comma before "and")
- Use "and" in full

Abelson, Robert P, Kurt P. Frey, and Aiden P. Gregg.
   Experiments with People. Etc...

More than three authors:
- First named author is listed followed by "et al." ("*et al.*" *refers to the Latin "and others"*). If there were a fourth author to *Experiments with People*, the reference would begin:

   Abelson, Robert P, et al.

Journals/periodicals

- Last name, first name of author.
- "Title of article."
- Name of publisher/publication:
   a. Monthly magazine:
      Publisher/publication.
   b. Weekly magazine & newspaper:
      Publisher/publication (no period)
      If the newspaper is not recognized put [location] to identify
   c. Journal paginated by volume/issue:
      Publisher/publication volume #.
      issue # (e.g. Volume 22 Issue 7 = 22.7)
- Date:
   a. Monthly magazine: Month year:
   b. Weekly magazine & newspaper:
      Day month year:
   c. Journal paginated by volume/issue:
      (Year):
- Page numbers:
   a. Monthly magazine: provide inclusive page numbers; i.e., 333-334. If item continued on other than the following page, list the start page and add "+". For example: 22+

APA

Multiple authors (up to 7):
- Name, initial(s)., separated by commas.
- Use "&" abbreviation instead of the word "and" before the name of the last author,

Abelson, R.P, Frey, K.P, & Gregg, A.P. (2010).

   Experiments with people. Etc...

Eight or more authors:
- List first six authors, insert three ellipsis points (...) followed by the name of the final author:

Journals/periodicals

- Last name, initial(s) of author.
- Date:
   a. Monthly magazine: (Year, month).
   b. Weekly magazine & newspaper: (Year, month day).
   c. Journal paginated by volume/issue: (Year).
- Title of article.
- *Name of publisher/publication*:
   a. Monthly/weekly magazine and newspaper: *Publisher/publication,* [Note: comma italicized]
   b. Journal paginated by volume/issue: *Publisher/publication, volume #* (issue #), (e.g. Volume 22 Issue 7 = 22 (7),) [Note: italicize only volume number, not issue number]
- Page #s: 333-334. [Except for newspapers & magazines, in which case the page numbers in your reference are preceded by 'p.' or 'pp.']

MLA

Article in a monthly magazine

Lublin, Nancy. "Jurassic Park Syndrome." *Fast Company*.
   Mar. 2009: 50. Print.

Article in a weekly magazine

Baker, Katie. "Why do IQ Scores Vary by Nation?" *Newsweek*
   2 Aug. 2010: 14. Print.

Article in a newspaper

Stackhouse, John. "Rock Stars, Africa and the Challenge to
   Canada." *Globe and Mail* [Toronto]10 May 2010: A3.
   Print.

Article in a journal paginated by volume

Ansell, Aaron. "Patronage in Northeast Brazil: The Political
   Value of Money in a Ritual Market." *American
   Anthropologist* 112.2 (2010): 283-294. Print.

Article in a journal paginated by issue

Napoleon, Val. "An Uncomfortable Discussion." *The Canadian
   Journal of Native Studies* 30.1 (2010): 45-48. Print.

DVD/Video

Nature: Hummingbirds – Magic in the Air. Prod. Fred
   Kaufman. WNET New York, 2010. DVD.

Motion Picture

The Producers. Dir. Susan Stroman. Prods. Mel Brooks and
   Jonathan Sanger. Universal Pictures. 2005. Film.

Music Recording

McLachlan, Sarah. "Loving You Is Easy." *Laws of Illusion*.
   Arista Records, 2010. CD.

APA

Article in a monthly magazine
Lublin, N. (2009, March). Jurassic Park syndrome.
Fast Company, 50.

Article in a weekly magazine
Baker, K. (2010, August 2). Why do IQ scores vary by nation?
Newsweek, p. 14.

Article in a newspaper
Stackhouse, J. (2010, May 10). Rock stars, Africa and the
challenge to Canada. *The Globe and Mail*, p. A3.

Article in a journal paginated by volume
Ansell, A. (2010). Patronage in Northeast Brazil: The political
value of money in a ritual market. *American
Anthropologist, 112* (2) 283-294.

Article in a journal paginated by issue
Napoleon, V. (2010). An uncomfortable discussion.
The Canadian Journal of Native Studies, 30 (1), 45-48.

DVD/Video
Kaufman, F. (Producer).
(2010). *Nature: Hummingbirds – Magic in the air*
[DVD]. New York, NY: WNET New York.

Motion Picture
Brooks, M. & Sanger, J. (Producers), & Stroman, S. (Director).
(2005). *The Producers* [Motion picture]. United States:
Universal Pictures.

Music Recording
McLachlan, S. (2010). Loving you is easy. On *Laws of Illusion*
[CD]. Montreal, QC: Arista Records.

MLA

Interviews/Conversations

a. Broadcast/published/formal
   - Name of person interviewed: Last name, first name
   - Title of interview (if any): in quotation marks
   - If interview published independently: *Italicize*
   - If no title, simply write "interview". You may add name of the interviewer if appropriate; i.e., Interview by (name of interviewer).
   - Bibliographic information
   - Provenance

Ramo, Joshua Cooper. Interview by Charlie Rose. *Charlie Rose*. PBS, New York. 11 May 2009. Television.

b. Personal
   - Name of the person interviewed
   - Type of interview: Personal interview/telephone interview
   - Date: day month year

Edwards, Connie. Telephone interview. 17 Oct. 2010.

Duhamel, Roger. Personal interview. 3 May 2011.

c. Email
   - Name of writer: Last name, first name.
   - Subject/topic: "in quotes".
   - Message to (name of person/organization)
   - Date: day month year
   - Provenance: Email

Laffoley, Eric. "Email subject lines." Message to the author. 27 Aug. 2010. Email.

APA

Interviews/Conversations

a. Broadcast/published/formal
    - Name of interviewee:
    - Date: (year, month day)
    - Content + name of interviewer
    - Bibliographic data

Ramo, J. C. (2009, May 11). [Interview by Charlie Rose
    of Joshua Cooper Ramo and his book *The Age of the
    Unthinkable*] New York: PBS

b. Personal Interview
Personal communications, such as interviews or emails
should be cited in text only. They are not included in the
reference list because they do not provide recoverable data.

c. Email
See "Personal interview" above.

MLA

Web-based documentation

In referencing a website, the following information should be included, if known:

- Author: Last name, first name. (Or director, compiler, editor, etc.)
- Title of work: (In *italics* if independent work. In "quotes" if part of a larger work.)
- Name of website: *italicized*
- Site owner or sponsor. n.p. (no publisher) if not known
- Publication date: day month year. n.d. (no date) if not known
- Provenance: Web.
- Date of access: day month year.

Kincaid, James R. "Tennyson's Major Poems: The Comic and Ironic Patterns." *Victorian Web*. The Victorian Web, 28 Mar. 2001. Web. 3 May 2011.

(Include a URL only when the reader cannot locate the source without it or when your instructor requires it. The URL follows the date of access and goes within <angle brackets> followed by a period.)

Print book in electronic format

Author: Last name, first name.
Title.
Place of publication: publisher, year of publication.
Title of database or website; italicized
Provenance. Date of access.

Friedman, Thomas L. *Hot, Flat, and Crowded*. New York: Farrar, Strauss and Giroux, 2008. *AvaxHome*. Web. 17 Mar. 2011.

APA

Web-based documentation

The rules for referencing a website are basically the same as for those in print. The following information should be included, if known:

- Author: Last name, initials. (Or director, compiler, editor, etc.)
- Date: (Year, month)
- Title of work
- *Title of publication*
- If DOI (Digital object identifier) assigned, use it.
- If no DOI, state; Retrieved from + URL information. (No retrieval date required.)

Kincaid, J R. (2001, March). Tennyson's Major Poems: The Comic and Ironic Patterns. *Victorian Web*. Retrieved from http://www.victorianweb.org/authors/tennyson/ kincaid/contents.html.

Print book in electronic format

Author: Last name, initials
Date: (year published)
Title
[Version]
Retrieval from + URL for site where available

Friedman, T.L. (2008). *Hot, flat, and crowded*. [si PDF version]. Retrieved from http://avaxhome.ws/ebooks/Politics_ Sociology/ Hot_Flat_Crowded.html

MLA

Periodical publication in an online database

Author: Last name, first name.
Title of article: "in quotation marks."
Name of the periodical (*italicized*).
Title of the database (*italicized*).
Medium of publication consulted (Web)
Date of access: Day month year

Schueller, Stephen M. "Promoting Wellness: Integrating
Community and Positive Psychology." *Journal of
Community Psychology* 37.7 (2009): 922-937. *Academic
Search Elite*. Web. 8 July 2010.

Digital Object Identifiers (DOIs)

MLA does not currently require DOI information as
documentation. Having said that, MLA encourages
researchers/students to include supplementary facts that
are relevant to their projects that they believe would be
useful to the reader. The addition would come at the end
of the entry in the works-cited list. There are two ways you
can do this:

Schueller, Stephen M. "Promoting Wellness: Integrating
Community and Positive Psychology." *Journal of
Community Psychology* 37.7 (2009): 922-937.
Academic Search Elite. Web. 8 July 2010. DOI: 10.1002/
jcop.20334.

Schueller, Stephen M. "Promoting Wellness: Integrating
Community and Positive Psychology." *Journal of
Community Psychology* 37.7 (2009): 922-937.
Academic Search Elite. Web. 8 July 2010.
<http://dx.doi.org/10.1002/jcop.20334>.

The URL in the second example should not be in color or
underlined in a printed paper.

APA

Periodical publication in an online database

Author: Last name, initials
Date: (year published)
Title of article
Name of journal & volume #:
Page range:
DOI:
If no DOI, include the URL for the journal's home page:
Retrieved from URL (no date required)

Schueller, S.M. (2009). Promoting wellness: integrating
community and positive psychology. *Journal of
Community Psychology, 37* (7), 922-937. doi: 10.1002/
jcop.20334

Organizing your work/having a good outline, pulls everything together so that you can write logically from start to finish

Outline objective

- Provide structure to write a solid first draft
- Great outline makes writing easier
- Clear on how assignment hangs together from start to finish
- Less likely to encounter writer's block

What determines your approach?
Must you:

- Describe a topic?
- Persuade someone of your point of view?
- Compare/contrast one system with another?
- Explain cause of something?
- Tell a story?
- Detail chronological events?

develop the organization/outline

INTRODUCTION

You've got your topic and you know what you want to prove about it. Now you have to organize it in a logical, step-by-step structure from opening paragraph to conclusion. Some call this an outline; others, simply organizing your work. It's a product of:

- Your topic/thesis
- Your research
- Your class notes
- Your own thinking

The number one objective of your outline is to give you the structure to write a solid first draft. Do a great outline, and the writing becomes a whole lot easier. There are a couple of other benefits:

- You're clear how your assignment hangs together from beginning to end
- You are less likely to encounter writer's block

Creating your organization or outline

This is where things can get tricky. You've got the topic, but what are you expected to do with it? Are you to:

- Describe what the topic is about?
- Persuade someone that your point of view is the right one?
- Compare one system with another?
- Explain why, when something happens, what the cause is?
- Tell a story, spelling out the major reasons why something happened and what it means?
- Provide a series of chronological events leading to a conclusion?

In other words, which approach are you to use?

Which approach will you use?

- Argumentative or Persuasive
- Cause and Effect
- Chronological
- Comparative
- Descriptive
- Expository
- Narrative
- Build to a climax
- Combination of approaches

Analytical

Read assignment material
and analyze what you've got:

- Brief descriptive of what you've read
- Your opinion, how you see the situation
- Support your arguments from text
- Develop conclusions

THE APPROACH TO USE TO BUILD YOUR CASE

Several approaches are available to show, tell, explain or prove to your readers what you want them to know. Your options include:

- Analytical
- Argumentative or Persuasive
- Cause and Effect
- Chronological
- Comparative
- Descriptive
- Expository
- Narrative
- Build to a climax
- Combination of approaches

Analytical

An analytical essay requires that you read assigned material; i.e., a literary text, a project, a report—and then analyze what you've got:

- Provide a brief description of what you've read.
- Give the reader your opinion, how you see the situation, your argument about the author's work, its strengths and shortcomings. Are there contradictions in what the author has said?
- Support your arguments with evidence from the written text.
- Develop your conclusions and tie those back to your analysis and thesis.

For example, suppose you're reviewing a report on the 2010 Winter Olympics in Vancouver. The report poses the question ***Should the Olympic Games be held in the same place every four years so as to keep costs down?***

Your argument (thesis) is that the Olympics should continue to be hosted by different countries. You discuss the issues raised by your point of view. Stated opinions might be:

- Yes, there are additional costs.
- Those costs are more than offset by the enthusiasm of the host nation and the new facilities that nation will acquire.

From your arguments and evidence, you draw your conclusions.

Argumentative/Persuasive

Convince reader that your point of view
is the right one:

- Be well informed about the situation
- Get supportive evidence
- Treat other arguments fairly
- Explain why you think you're right
- Build your case – weaker points first, leading to strongest

Cause and Effect

How one thing is the cause
of another:

- Be fair and stay neutral
- Discuss alternatives
- Let reader draw conclusions

Argumentative or Persuasive

Your job is to convince your reader that your point of view on a particular situation or issue is the right one. In order to do that you must be:

- Very well informed about the situation or issue
- Aware of what the literature might have to say. In your approach you:
  - Marshal the evidence to support your case.
  - Take the time to explain the other arguments and their legitimacy and treat them fairly.
  - Explain why you think yours is the right solution and deserves the support of the reader
  - Build to a climax with your points; i.e., begin with weakest points and end with the strongest.

For example: You think the Olympic Games are a waste of time and money. Surely issues of poverty and concerns for the environment should have a much higher priority.

You take what you know, support it with your research, evaluate the opinions of others, and develop your conclusions, all with one aim – to convince others of the validity of your argument.

Cause and Effect

You present an argument about how one thing is the cause of another. Whatever you do, you need to:

- Be fair
- Discuss alternatives openly
- Stay neutral, don't bias the reader
- Let readers draw their own conclusions

The question being raised is **What caused something to happen?** And **What was the effect or impact of that?**

For example: The Olympic Games. On one hand they provide a city and country with incredible new facilities for future use. They give athletes a chance to shine. They help encourage fitness. On the other hand the Games cost vast sums of money; taxes must be increased to pay for them. The Games disrupt normal life and often displace people. They produce traffic jams. Prices, especially food and accommodation, go through the roof.

Chronological

Talk about sequence of events
- Describe the situation
- Identify each event
- Impact of event in forwarding the action
- Interpretation of event's importance
- Your conclusions

Comparative

Compare the same things, contrast different things:
- Identify differences and similarities
- Draw conclusions
- Use a chart to help you

Chronological

You talk about the sequence of events. For example, if your topic was the 2010 BP oil spill in the Gulf of Mexico, you'd identify each event as it occurred, identifying the actual date and time. Here is a possible scenario for the BP oil spill:

- Describe the situation prior to the event

- Describe initial event (explosion) and what led to it

- The impact of the event in forwarding action:
  - Initial responses
  - Longer term responses

- Political, economic and environmental implications

- Your interpretation and that of others of the event's importance

- Your conclusions

Comparative

Use a comparative approach if asked to compare or contrast one system with another:

- *Comparing* occurs between the same things. For example, apples and apples

- *Contrasting* occurs between two different things. For example, apples and oranges

With this approach the focus is on similarities and differences. You're identifying what those differences are and what they mean. You might find it of value to use a chart to make the comparisons.

For example: *Compare* your bike with your friend's bike. What are the similarities and what are the differences?

Contrast a bike with a car, or to be very different, with a horse and cart.

You draw your conclusions.

Descriptive

You describe something:
- Provide sufficient detail
- What's your viewpoint?
- What do others think?
- Merits of each point of view
- Your conclusions

Expository

Shine a light as detailed as possible on an event/situation:
- Unbiased description
- Help reader understand the circumstances
- Analyze but don't judge
- Use present tense

Descriptive

You're asked to describe something. It could be a person, an event, a place, a book. In your writing you want to capture this as clearly and in as much detail as possible so that your reader can closely experience what you're describing. In other words try and make it interesting – brainstorm it – think outside the box.

As part of your description you need to provide:
- Your specific viewpoint
- The viewpoints of others
- The merits of each point of view
- Your conclusions

For example, a group of friends have gone to see a movie. You didn't like it much while some of your friends thought it was great.
- You state what you liked/disliked about the movie and why.
- You tell us what your friends thought and why.
- You consider the merits of both viewpoints.
- Finally you draw your own conclusions, based on the various points of view.

Expository

Expository means to shed light on something. What an expository essay does is lay out in detail as much information as possible about a certain event or situation. The objective is to provide readers with a thorough, unbiased descriptive of this situation/event so that they understand the circumstances surrounding it.

To make sure the presentation is fresh, the writer uses the present tense.

For example, if you're asked to come up with an expository essay on the Winter Olympics, what facts and opinions would you provide your readers? Remember:
- You're not trying to prove anything. You are simply laying out all the facts and opinions.
- You can analyze the event/situation as long as you don't judge or criticize it.
- You can explore the event/situation as deeply as you wish as long as you present your conclusions fairly.

Narrative

A story that follows a particular theme or pattern:

- Provide background
- Organize chronologically
- Begin with earliest sequence
- Show how events flow over time
- Your conclusions

Build to a climax

- Begin with least important step
- Add progressively bigger steps
- End with climactic step

Combine different approaches

The best approach may in fact be a combination of approaches

Narrative

A narrative is a story that follows a particular theme or pattern. It could be personal, it could be historical. Either way the story means something to the writer and is often a sequence of events tied to a particular theme.

In the construction of your narrative, you:
• Follow a particular theme
• Provide any background readers need to know
• Organize in chronological order
• Begin with the earliest sequence
• Show how time flows through your transitions from one event to another
• Draw your conclusions

Your story can be about your own experiences. For example, if you went to the Olympics you could write about that. If you went on vacation you could describe that trip, what you enjoyed about it, what you didn't, and what you may have learned about yourself.

You might then draw conclusions as to whether it was something you'd do again, or whether next time you'd do things differently.

The following two categories apply to most of the approaches we've covered:

Build to a climax

Take your topic and proceed as follows:
• Begin with the least important steps
• Add progressively bigger steps, each building on the previous step
• End with the climactic step, built upon those that have gone before and leading to your conclusions. For example, in preparing to run a marathon you start with short training runs, add in longer endurance runs, and end with the climactic step itself: the big race.

Reality: Combining different approaches

Usually one approach will be combined with elements of another. For example, a chronological essay or narrative can easily build to a climax, each event getting bigger and bigger, just as in running a marathon.

How to create the logical sequence for writing the draft; some possibilities include:

- In your head
- Write out a list
- Use index cards

PULL THE INFORMATION TOGETHER IN A LOGICAL, STEP-BY-STEP FORMAT

Once you have decided which approach to use, assemble the information you've gathered into the step-by-step, linear format the essay or term paper requires. This sequencing builds your case and its supporting arguments from introduction to conclusion.

For some, this step-by-step format is a very formal outline. For others it's less formal and more loosely organized. There is no right or wrong way to do this. The only result you're after is a logical sequence that you can then put down on paper.

It also depends on the type and scope of the project. For example, a major term paper with multiple source documents is handled very differently from a short essay dealing with less information.

It also depends on you. How do you like to handle things? Do you like to do things visually, such as with large mind maps? Do you prefer to use word processing or spreadsheet software to get organized?

Here are some possibilities to consider:

In your head. Some people, especially if it's a short essay, simply do it in their head. They know what they want to say — it's easy for them to simply write the whole essay.

Write out a list. List the key items down on a piece of paper, from class notes to class texts and research. Against each item you might note the supporting arguments and evidence that builds your case. Move these items around as needed to develop a logical sequence, then number them. It's easy to do using a word processor or spreadsheet.

Use index cards. Prior to computers, organizing each item on an index card was a preferred method. For some people, it still is. You can color code items by topic sub-categories or use different colored cards.

You next sort the cards to sequence them and number them. It's easy enough to lay cards out on a table – or the floor – and shift them around into the desired sequence.

Logical sequence for writing the draft (cont.)

- Use a database
- Use a mind map/sticky notes

Once you have your sequence...

Lay out the basic structure

- Introduction
- Main body
- Summary or conclusion

Use a database. A computer database is another way in which you can first store information, sort it and arrange it in sequence for writing. You may find this particularly suitable if you have a major term paper to produce that requires storing a lot of information.

Use a mind map or similar techniques. Making use of a mind map or sticky notes system is a great way to organize your information. For example, the seven priorities established in the analysis of "Health Care in a Developing World" (p. 37), is ideal for the writing sequence.

POST SEQUENCE –
LAY OUT THE BASIC STRUCTURE

Once you have your sequence, you can lay out the basic structure of the blocks that make up the essay or term paper. We've deliberately kept this step separate from the last major step (Pull the information together in a logical, step-by-step format) so that you can see the two distinct processes.

In reality, these last two steps are often done simultaneously; i.e. when you're organizing, you can put the items you're going to be discussing into the essay blocks to which they belong. It's often the most efficient way to organize your work.

The basic structure or blocks that make up the essay or term paper are:

- An introduction/opening section

- Main body

- Summary or conclusion

The body part expands as needed to accommodate more key topic points, more information, more evidence – all in support of proving your point – your thesis.

The Five Paragraph Essay

- Introductory paragraph
- Three body paragraphs
- Conclusion paragraph

Introductory paragraph
- Sets up topic
- Sets the tone
- Sets up what you intend to prove (your thesis)

That opening paragraph should also:
- Prepare reader for what is to come
- Grab the reader's attention

THE FIVE PARAGRAPH ESSAY: WHERE IT ALL STARTS

Many students get introduced to essay writing with the five paragraph essay. Every other essay is simply an expansion of this format.

The five paragraph essay consists of:

1. Introductory paragraph

2. Three body paragraphs

3. Conclusion paragraph

Introductory paragraph

- Sets up the topic you're discussing

- Sets the tone for the reader (you need to know who your reader is and what they expect from you)

- Sets up what you want to prove and claim about the topic – your thesis.

You may prefer to wait until the body of the essay is written, or at least thought about, before finalizing your introduction. By waiting, you often develop a more complete picture of the issue, giving you insights for a better and more compelling introduction.

The opening paragraph should prepare the reader for what is to come. It should also, wherever possible, start with some means of grabbing the reader's attention and retaining that attention.

Body paragraphs

- Introduce topic sentence
- Explain why it's important
- Give supporting evidence
- Provide effective transition links

Conclusion paragraph

- Confirms opening statement
- Restates the thesis
- Asserts closing position

Body paragraphs

Set out the three strongest, most compelling points you want to make to support your thesis; i.e., one compelling point per paragraph.

1. Introduce the topic sentence

2. Explain why you think it's such an important point

3. Support your claim with evidence, whether that's from the text you've been working on, or statistics or whatever proof you have.

4. Link the paragraph to the one before it and the one after so there's a smooth transition between them.

Linking – linking isn't just for websites. It's for connecting not just these three paragraphs together but the introduction and conclusion to the body of the essay.

Be sure that easy transitions mark your journey from one paragraph to another.

Conclusion paragraph

The conclusion confirms what was said in the opener, restates the thesis, and then boldly asserts that closing position. I like to loop back to what was said in the opening paragraph and the thesis to complete what I've written.

Complex Academic Papers

Issues of synthesis and analysis

More components to be dealt with:
- More information
- More arguments
- More proof
- More connections

Introduction
- Introduce topic
- Give background
- State your thesis
- May require several paragraphs, depending on length and complexity of topic

FIVE-PARAGRAPH ESSAY TO COMPLEX ACADEMIC PAPER: MAKING THE JUMP

The prevailing wisdom

"Most (students) can prepare a basic outline, but to take material from numerous sources and synthesize it into coherent paragraphs that focus on a particular theme is difficult. Usually, they will write a paragraph about information contained in one report, then another paragraph/report. Synthesis is hard for them, especially when academic writing demands that they also provide their educated opinion!"

Canadian Nursing Faculty, July 2009

"Recent analyses indicate that more than 50 percent of first-year college students are unable to produce papers relatively free of language errors. Analyzing arguments and synthesizing information are also beyond the scope of most first-year students."

National Commission on Writing in America's Schools and Colleges, April 2003

Issues of synthesis and analysis are a problem for many students.

And yet, the basic essay format remains the same – it's just that there are many more components to be dealt with and incorporated into your work – more information, more arguments, more proof, more connections.

Introduction/Opening Section

- Introduce your topic

- Give background

- State what you intend to prove (your thesis).

- Depending on the length or complexity of your work, this could be as little as a single paragraph – or multiple paragraphs over several pages.

Main Body

- Two to four sections
- Section for each major argument
- Break section into paragraphs required to set out the argument
- Create flow

Conclusion

- Set out your conclusion to prove your thesis
- Use as many paragraphs as necessary

Main Body

The length of the main body will depend on the number of major arguments, ideas and concepts you plan to introduce and the material to support them. Some suggest that it be from two to four sections as follows:

- Allocate a section to each major argument or concept you plan to discuss.

- Break the section up into the number of paragraphs required by the argument. It might only be a couple of paragraphs. It could be as many as a dozen or more.

- In laying out your headings, check to make sure that flow exists from one part to another. If it doesn't, move your information around until it does. If you use sticky notes or index cards, they're easy to shift until you get a sequence/structure that works for you.

Your goal is to create flow - where the conclusions of one paragraph lead or bridge to the next paragraph or section.

Conclusion

The length depends on the amount of material to be covered. It could be no more than a couple of paragraphs. If there are a dozen key points to be summarized, the paragraph count will go up. The objective is to set out your conclusions in such a way as to prove your thesis.

In Step 8, "Complete the first draft," the development of the structure is described in more detail.

Outline for complex issues

The overall picture is derived from several sources. Can you grasp this overall picture?

Can you connect the dots between various materials/sources?
- Do your sources interconnect? If so, how?
- What is the impact?

Ask yourself:
- How does one thing connect to another – or several "anothers"?
- Do they go together?
- Does combining these connections result in a more powerful or compelling argument?
- Is synergy at work here?

DEVELOPING AN OUTLINE FOR COMPLEX ISSUES

The overall picture

Can you grasp the overall picture? After all your research, mind mapping, brainstorming and freewriting, the questions you've asked, the sources you've tapped, the evidence you've found, do you understand and appreciate the complete scenario?

According to instructors, students have a tendency *not to connect the dots between various materials*. For example, you may have been researching an issue and have half a dozen sources that validate what you're saying. Too many students treat each of these sources as separate entities, each needing its own paragraph. That may be valid. However, it's much more likely that these sources interconnect; one thing affecting another, confirming information from a completely different source, or an interview you've carried out.

Instructors want to see students analyzing and making these connections. So, as a student, ask yourself these questions:

- How does one thing connect with another or several anothers?

- Do they go together?

- Can they combine to make a more compelling point or argument than if split into separate entities?

In the real world, things have a habit of working synergistically; several components working together often produce a better result than each component on its own. A nursing team assigned to the care of a group of patients will probably do a better job than individual nurses assigned to those same patients. The communication will be better, the overall plan for the patient will be better coordinated and adhered to – all leading to a more positive outcome for the patient.

This same kind of realization can be true for your writing. What conclusions can you draw when several different sources are contributing to the end result?

Effective "rough" outline

When lots of material is involved:

- Split into sections
- Split sections into paragraphs
- Use mind maps/sticky notes/index cards to move material to where it has a logical fit
- Use this rough outline to create a finished outline from which to write the first draft

Work in chunks

- Chunks can make working with a lot of material more manageable
- Just deal with one area, or one section, or one paragraph at a time
- Working in chunks allows you to focus

Effective outline: rough one first

It's asking a lot to come up with a finished outline right off the bat, so don't even try. Go for a rough outline instead. Here are some suggestions:

- When you have a lot of material:
    - Split it into sections
    - Split it further into paragraphs pertaining to each section

- Use sticky notes or index cards to move the material around until you're satisfied that it's in the right place or sequence. (Mind maps work well here.)

- Prepare a finished outline from your rough one as the basis for writing your first draft.

Work in chunks

When dealing with a lot of material, different reports, web references, various records, it can become unmanageable. If you break it into chunks, however, make sure you concentrate solely on the chunk and deal with all the elements it contains. A chunk can be a section, a paragraph, sometimes even a sentence.

In my experience, this chunking process is a lot easier and less frustrating than trying to handle several areas at once. Pay attention to the following:

- What topic question are you dealing with?

- What research goes with it?

- What other information?

- What opinions?

- What arguments?

- What proofs?

- How does it fit together?

- Are there connections with other sections that you need to note?

Don't rush to write

- Put yourself on pause and do all the important up-front stuff (Remember Step 3 dealing with Discovery)
- Remember to schedule time in your calendar to do this work

Instructors want your opinion. It counts. So be bold – give it!

I like working with chunks because it's very focused. If you try it, I suggest that you work one chunk and then another. In this way, the scope of your project may not seem as massive or daunting.

Once all chunks are done, take an overall look at the picture. You might even try a mind map showing each outline chunk, where it connects with other chunks, in what sequence, and the conclusions you might draw.

(Chunks also work very well in developing your drafts and editing them. More on that in Steps 8 and 9).

Don't Rush to Write

This point is too important to ignore. You're pressed for time and your mind says *I've got to get writing*.

Don't. Remember Step 3 and the importance of doing the up-front work? Even if you have very little time, do what you can because when you rush to write you miss important things, critical connections. Your research, your extra reading, re-examining class notes – it's all part of the up-front work.

If you can, schedule the hours in your calendar to do this work well. It's a great habit to acquire, pays dividends now, and can make a huge difference to your future career.

The Importance of Your Opinion

I want to add one more thing into the outline mix – your opinion. Where an opinion is called for it's important for you to step out and say what you think. Your opinion counts. Based on the text, your research and its analysis, the interviews, other things you've read - what is your opinion? The reader wants to know.

Remember this: The work you do here will pay dividends throughout your career, not just while you are in school or college.

Tips

- Treat every argument fully, regardless of how short or how weak it may appear
- In your work, you may wish to consider going from general to specific

Summary

Right now, as you're preparing to write, you're probably wondering whether all this is worth it. Some of you may think – well I'll never have to use this again.

The odds are that you will – that someone will want you to write a report for them, or a proposal, or a screenplay. You might want to do an analysis of a videogame you've thought up, or an iPhone application, or a business you want to start. The principles are the same. The tools like mind mapping and brainstorming will serve you amazingly well. Use them now, while you're in school or college, and get accustomed to using them. They'll benefit your whole career.

TIPS FOR ORGANIZING YOUR WORK

Treat each argument comprehensively and thoroughly

Just because one argument is shorter than another, or seemingly less important, still treat it fully. Build your case, however, by starting with weaker arguments and adding stronger and stronger ones.

Go from general to specific

In discussing Step 3, "Come up with the Right Topic", I spoke of the value of limiting the topic by going from general to specific. In organizing your work it may also help to go from general to specific.

Suppose your outline involves the average number of hours children watch television per week. You could:

• Begin in *general* terms

• Zero in on a *specific* factor

For example, a general factor might be that "more and more parents are concerned that their children are watching too much television."

This could lead to a specific factor such as "the need to prevent children from watching programs that contain violence."

121

Save that draft outline! It may contain an idea worth saving

Track your work

When you've completed your organization or outline, ask yourself:

- Does everything relate to my thesis?
- Does it flow?

Save that draft

Don't pitch that draft just yet. There may be an idea or two worth keeping – or a way of saying something that works well that you don't want to lose.

Tracking your work

How long is the essay you're writing? How many words? How many pages? Is it to be double spaced? What is the preferred font and font size? Check for word count in software like MS Word by going to Tools and checking under Word Count.

COMPLETING YOUR ORGANIZATION/ OUTLINE

Once you've completed your organization or outline, go through it and ask yourself:

- Does each section relate to my thesis?

- Does each section flow from beginning to end, point by point, argument by argument, paragraph by paragraph?

If you're well organized, whether in outline form or some other structure, writing the actual draft will prove much easier to accomplish.

Write with your reader in mind

(Step 7)

Complete the first draft

(Step 8)

Revise and edit the draft

(Step 9)

Take one last look

(Step 10)

THE WRITING STEPS

There are four Writing Steps. They are:

- Write with your reader in mind

- Complete the first draft

- Revise and edit the draft

- Take one last look

Step 7 often gets overlooked. A screenwriter writes for the movie audience. A sports reporter writes for sports fans. You are writing for your professor, instructor, lecturer, board of examiners.

It's very important to keep the specific audience in mind from the start. If you know them well and are aware of what they are expecting, tailor your topic, and how you present it, to that audience.

Steps 8 and 9 logically follow one another. First you write the draft, then revise the content as necessary. Finally you polish the revised draft through editing and proofreading.

Step 10 is the pause before handing in your work. It's that last chance to step back and think about what you've created. Are you happy with it? Should any final changes be made?

Put yourself in your reader's shoes so as to understand who they are

Think about what your reader expects from you

write with your
reader in mind

WHO IS YOUR READER?

In business, one of the things you learn is to put yourself in your customer's shoes. If literally you sell sports shoes, and a customer wants a pair of runners, you'll ask questions like what kind of running and how far, what kind of terrain, how much support, weight of the shoe, as well as price.

Start thinking about your readers in that way. Put yourself in their shoes. Who are they? Is your reader your instructor, or is it someone else? What do you know about them, their thinking, their expectations, that would help you write with them in mind?

WHAT YOUR READER EXPECTS FROM YOU

Your reader wants to know that you can take a topic and, through your writing, show that you:

- Fully understand and can think about it

- Have done the required research, identified other points of view and can discuss each of them

- Are able to use the evidence you gathered through your studies, research, etc., to convincingly present your arguments

- Can express and justify your own view in light of the opinion of others, including that of your reader. It's very important that you take a strong stand with your opinion.

- Are able to write in a manner that reflects the language, tone and professional discipline of your area of study

*Think about what
you want your reader
to remember*

*Get feedback from
others to see if what
you've written will work
for your reader*

WHAT YOU WANT YOUR READER TO REMEMBER

- That you set up your thesis and proved it

- That you explained what had to be explained, avoiding assumptions

- That you were effective at using the evidence you found to construct your arguments clearly and concisely

- That your own opinions and conclusions were clearly expressed

- The two or three major points you made, even when the detail of your work has been forgotten

Test drive what you write

Before you hand in your work, try it on for size with someone else – preferably an independent reader who has no vested interest in you one way or another. Friends may work, as may parents, provided they're willing to be honest. What you're looking for is feedback. Does what I've written work for my audience? Does it flow? Are assumptions or quantum leaps being made? Are there holes big enough to drive a truck through?

This kind of rehearsal is extremely valuable, if you're willing and have the time to do it. It invariably makes for a better final product *focused on the reader*.

Always work from your organization/outline and thesis

Use wide margins & double spacing and/or comply with APA/MLA format.

Begin with the basics:

1. Introduce the topic
2. Give some background
3. What you intend to prove (your thesis statement)

So you're blocked. Now what?

- You may need to take a break
- You may need to talk to someone

complete the first draft

Your work is organized/outlined. You have your thesis. You're ready to begin the first draft.

As you write, *keep checking your organization/outline and thesis to make sure you're on track.*

Give yourself plenty of space on each page to make corrections. I recommend at least a three inch margin, plus double or triple spacing. You could, of course, simply use APA/MLA or other designated format for your draft.

HOW TO BEGIN

Introducing the topic

The first thing we normally do is introduce the topic, give some background/history about it, why that particular topic was chosen and what we intend to prove about it (thesis).

Now – one of the things we all like to do is come up with a dynamic opening paragraph. Sometimes we can produce it right off the top. We get the correct phrasing, or the analogy is perfect, or it just works. Too often, however, we try for a winning paragraph and however hard we try, nothing works. We keep struggling because the opening is so important. It sets the tone. If we're blocked, however, those efforts are probably pointless.

A suggestion: *Wait till you've done the closing paragraph.* It can be easier to write an opening paragraph when you are clear about the conclusion to your work. In other words, your closing paragraph may give a far better answer as to how that opening paragraph should look and what it should contain.

What to do if you're blocked

If it's not an essay in class and you're at home, maybe you need to take a break and do something else. If you're not in an exam room, you might talk to a friend or your instructor. They may have some insights for you.

Writing strategies if blocked

(especially by that opening paragraph)

- Write the basics
- Jump into what you know (part of the middle section, whatever) as long as you keep going
- Do the end notes and bibliography

You can always return to the opening paragraph, or wherever else you were blocked, later on

But what if you are in an exam room, or it's midnight and the essay has to be handed in at ten the next morning? Here are some suggestions on how to proceed:

Write the basic information

Don't attempt a winning paragraph for the moment. Instead, keep it simple. Just write the basic information your reader needs to know: What your topic is about and what you intend to prove. "My topic is about Hamlet's state of mind and I intend to prove, through my research and my analysis of Shakespeare's text, that he was sane."

As I mentioned earlier, sometimes it's smart to wait until you've done your closing paragraph and then return to the opener to determine exactly what you want to say, when things are clearer. At that time, you might want to think like an ad copywriter:

How can I **hook** my readers so that they're intrigued by what I have to say and want to read on?

The hook may give you an interesting lead in – even a provocative one.

Jump into what you do know

Another thing you could do is jump into what you do know. If you're confident about those middle paragraphs, start working with them. That still keeps you moving forward. You can go back and make the connections to the opening paragraph later.

Do the end notes and bibliography

Get the end notes and bibliography out of the way so that you don't have to think about them on completing your assignment.

*For each main body
section argument/idea:*

- Present idea/concept
- Debate it
- Draw your conclusion
- Bridge to the text

*Paragraphs may consist
of a few sentences,
or several, depending
on complexity*

*Each sentence must move
the action forward and
relate to each other*

BEYOND THE OPENING PARAGRAPH

Writing the main sections

Once the opening paragraph or paragraphs are done you proceed to write the two to four sections that contain the major arguments, concepts and ideas to support your thesis. These sections consist of a single paragraph or a series of paragraphs. The more complex, the more sections and paragraphs you are likely to need.

Each section deals with a new idea or concept from your organization/outline. Each paragraph deals with a sub-topic within that section. Your job is to develop and work your descriptions and arguments concerning this idea or concept through to completion. The sequence is:

- Present the idea/concept
- Debate the pros and cons
- Draw your conclusions
- Bridge or transition to the next section/paragraph

Paragraphs & sentences – your building blocks

A paragraph may be as few as three or four sentences to as many as ten or fifteen. Use as many sentences as you need to illustrate the idea/concept.

The first sentence in a paragraph introduces the second. The second refers back to the first and introduces the third and so on. These sentences provide full or sustained development. It's like a knit pattern. If it doesn't connect, it will unravel and the reader won't be able to progress "with you." (*You want the reader to follow what you've said and understand it the first time around, effortlessly.*)

Finally you have a sentence, or sentences, which create *closure* for that paragraph as well as being the hook to the next paragraph and a bridge or transition to the next idea/concept.

135

*Each section must be
complete in itself*

*Synthesis – how well

or in what way do all

the components of your

work fit together?*

If you're writing a business essay instead of an academic subject, I suggest that you avoid overly long paragraphs. It's often easier to get your point across with a fresh paragraph than to make an existing paragraph too long or complex. This may also be valid for academic purposes.

Make sure each section is complete in itself

Each section you write must be complete in itself. Key ideas and arguments are always presented and debated, and conclusions are drawn. It's important, however, that you show your reader how these conclusions lead or bridge naturally to the next idea in your organization/ outline. This becomes the next section ... and so on.

The importance of synthesis

We've already gone through this in Step 6 but the point needs to be reinforced here. You are likely dealing with topics with increased complexity. You'll have gathered a lot of information from various sources. Now, how does all this information fit together? How does one section impact another? Are there connections between areas that you hadn't appreciated before. What, if anything, does this change?

By synthesizing the information in this manner, you gain a much broader perspective on the topic, on the situation or question you're facing, and your work will reflect it.

TIPS

- Let your writing flow
- Stay focused
- Keep checking your outline and thesis
- Remember your reader
- Write in chunks
- Apply the K.I.S.S. principle to help keep writing clear and easily understood

OTHER USEFUL TIPS

Let the writing flow

In this first cut at your work, minimize editing. Too much editing impedes flow and tends to hinder progress. It's more important to get your ideas down on paper so you can examine them and play around with them. Don't worry if you write too much. You can always revise or edit later.

Stay focused

Keep checking your outline and thesis

Don't forget your reader

Can your reader follow your arguments, descriptions, analysis and conclusions? If not, what might you have to change?

Try Writing in Chunks

As a writer, I have found it incredibly useful to work in chunks. A chunk can be a section, a paragraph, a page, even a sentence that you decide to work on intensively in order to get it the way you want. The chunk often deals with a specific sub-topic – but frankly it can be any area that gives you some kind of problem or challenge and would benefit from total focus.

Just make sure than when you've completed work on the chunk that it fits with what came before and what comes after.

Remember the K.I.S.S. principle

The K.I.S.S. principle stands for "Keep It Simple, Students!" Though more of a business term, the K.I.S.S. principle can be very useful in writing, especially if you're writing about topics that deal with business or the economy.

The rationale behind the K.I.S.S. principle is that we often make things more complicated than they need to be.

- Fully develop what you're working on:
  - complete the discovery process
  - do enough research
  - avoid writing based on skimpy material, irrelevant material, or duplication

- Beware of jargon

In our writing that can mean:

- Explanations that are too intricate and long-winded

- Sentences that are overly long and complex

If you can construct your arguments simply and clearly, using less words rather than more and shorter sentences rather than longer ones, they're often:

- Easier to follow

- More likely to be understood

- More likely to be remembered.

The opposite to K.I.S.S. may also be true

Academic writing tends to follow more complex patterns than writing for business. Sentence structure tends to be longer, avoiding bullet points and short sentences and phrases.

Failure to do enough research with discovery

Instructors are often concerned that students stop the discovery process too soon and don't fully develop what they're working on. This is particularly true with research. Too many students write a 2,000 word essay on skimpy material. Because they haven't done enough research they try to fudge through it, duplicating what they've said and filling in with irrelevant material.

The message? Do the up-front work necessary to uncover solid material, ideas and arguments to support what you're saying.

Inappropriate jargon

Use the specific language of a discipline if that's your area of study and your reader is familiar with it. Otherwise it comes across as jargon, or worse, talking down. Based on the K.I.S.S. principle, avoid it.

When you reach your conclusions, ask yourself:

- Does everything flow?
- Does it support my thesis?

Make sure the conclusions you draw are your own

Consider linking your conclusions back to the opening paragraph

REACHING CONCLUSIONS

All your ideas, descriptions and arguments are down on paper. You're about to write your final paragraph. Ask yourself:

- Does everything I've written flow logically to this point?

- Does it support my thesis?

Your overall conclusions are built step by step on the conclusions derived from each individual section. It may support your thesis to restate these individual section findings prior to setting down your overall conclusions.

Make sure that the conclusions are yours, not somebody else's (even though others may agree with you). You want your reader to know that they've been reached based on your classwork, your research, your studies and, above all, your own thinking.

Link back to your opening paragraph

I like to tie my conclusions back to the statements made in the opening paragraph. For me, it connects the beginning and the end, making the work whole and complete. For example, let's say your topic was about the impact of television on children. In your introduction you said, *When I was a kid, my parents allowed us to watch anything as long as we were in bed by eight-thirty.*

Based on your findings that unsupervised television and computer/Internet usage leads to undesirable attitudes or exposure to impressionable images, you might conclude that *I wish my parents had done things differently. I recommend that today's parents exhibit greater care in what they allow their children to watch.* This connects the beginning of your work with the end.

If your thesis does not work, re-evaluate it

When you've finished writing:

- Read what you've written out loud
- Note where major changes may be required
- Make minor changes (if easy to do)
- Set the draft aside and return to it later. This often gives you a fresh perspective on what you've written.

What if your thesis doesn't pan out?

Any time you realize that your thesis won't work, stop and see what will. An unworkable thesis has no value. Not only will your grades suffer, but so will your self-esteem. Even though it means extra work, take the proactive step and rework it.

YOUR CONCLUSIONS ARE WRITTEN. NOW WHAT?

You've put your pen down. You've hit save for the last time. What's next?

Read what you've written out loud

Reading out loud gives you a sense of how well your essay or term paper works. It will also tell you where changes are required. (Step 9 details the benefits of reading out loud.) If you're not good at reading out loud, get someone else to read while you listen. Or record yourself, and play it back.

Mark on the draft where major reworking or additional input is required, or where something needs to be deleted.

Consider making minor changes as part of the first draft rather than leaving them for the revision stage.

Once you've made any initial changes, set the draft aside. If you can leave it for a day or two, you can come back to it refreshed. You might also want to discuss your efforts with friends, or in a writing lab in order to get additional feedback.

First revise the content,
then edit what
you've written

revise and edit
the draft

Writers often say that writing is rewriting. My experience is that the more successful the up-front work, the less rewriting or revision your work will require. That's the payoff for all the prewriting, research, and topic exploration.

STEP 9 HAS TWO PARTS...
REVISION AND EDITING

1. *Revision* comes first and deals with content. What do You need to change about the content? There are a number of reasons for this:

   - You have new information to incorporate

   - Old information is not relevant and should be deleted

   - Your understanding of a situation changes and the writing needs to reflect it. (This might include a change in your thesis.)

   - The sequencing of what you've written doesn't work and has to be altered

2. *Editing and proofreading* follows revision. This is where you deal with the style and tone of what you've written. You change words and phrases, and shift things around to fit better. It doesn't alter the content. The result is a work more clearly and fluidly written, so that the reader can fully understand and appreciate what you're trying to say and prove.

(When you revise, you're also editing so there's no hard and fast rule here. However, once revision is complete, focus on the editing.)

*Reading out loud helps
answer key questions:*

- Is anything missing?
- Does your work hang together?
- Does the overall impression work?
- Is the work focused and on track?
- Are sections complete in themselves?
- Does it flow?

Why you should read your work out loud

- *You won't miss anything.* Reading to yourself, it's easy to miss a left out word, incorrect use of grammar, a sentence without a verb, etc. Reading out loud usually picks up these errors.

- *It gives you some idea of whether your work hangs together or not.* It tells you if something's missing in the content. Are there unexplained gaps? Are there unproved assumptions? Is the reader asked to accept giant leaps of faith? All these get flagged as areas to work on.

- *It gives you an overall impression of your essay or term paper* – where it works, where it doesn't and where you need to spend more time.

- *It tells you if your work is focused and on track.* Does everything you've written pertain to your thesis? Where it doesn't, mark it for further attention.

- *It helps you assess if each section produces a cogent argument or description.* Is each section complete in itself? If not, what must you do to change and/or improve it?

- *It tells you if your writing flows.* Does one sentence flow to the next? Does one paragraph lead to another? If the paragraphs don't connect, what kind of bridge is required to join them? Is a word, a phrase, sentence, or paragraph in the wrong place? Is something missing entirely?

More reasons for reading out loud:

- Have you repeated yourself?
- Is the tone consistent?
- Did you avoid jargon?
- Did you avoid junk or garbage?
- Does it stimulate the desire to read on?

- *You know if you've repeated yourself.* Is what you've said redundant? Have you used the same word or phrasing too often, or one right after the other?

- *Consistency of tone.* Is the tone used throughout your work consistent, and will it appeal to your reader? Reading out loud identifies where the tone is off.

- *You avoid junk or garbage.* When you read what you've written, keep your junk meter on. What do I mean by that? Imagine that you have an alarm that goes off whenever you hear the following:

  - gross generalizations

  - assumptions that can't be proven

  - excessive wordiness

  - writing that sounds great but has little or nothing to do with the topic

  As you read, ask yourself "Does this thought, this paragraph, this word belong in my work? Is it junk? Is it garbage?" If you have any doubts, strike it out!

- *It brings your work off the page.* Does your work come alive when read? Can you feel it? Does it draw some kind of emotional response? The best writing comes alive because it's written in a way that doesn't leave the work too dry and flat:

  - it sounds right

  - it has energy

  - it flows

  - it stimulates

  Your style, the words and phrases you use, and the compelling quality of your arguments all have a lot to do with it. Do these elements inform the reader? Do they stimulate the desire to keep on reading?

*Editing in chunks
allows you to:*

- Focus on a specific segment
- Work that segment intensively

FINAL POINTS

Once you have highlighted the areas for revision, rework your text until you're satisfied with the content and the arguments you've put together to support your thesis.

When revision is done, edit your work. Follow the recommendations we've already made concerning tone, flow, language.

Edit in Chunks

In Step 8, Complete The First Draft, I spoke about writing in chunks. It can also be very useful and helpful to edit in chunks. Editing in chunks is manageable and a great alternative to the overwhelming effort often required in editing a complete document all at once.

I apply this strategy to any area of text that's giving me trouble and needs to be straightened out. Applying this process provides me with two things:

1. It lets me focus on a specific segment without having to think about any other area of the material

2. It lets me work the segment intensively. When you've locked yourself into a chunk of a few paragraphs it's open for exploration. This is especially important if you believe that the content needs expanding or further explanation. It also permits the reverse. If you've got too much material you can cut it down to the size you need. If you've got more than one version of the material, as I sometimes do, where you must incorporate everything into one document, editing in chunks may be your answer.

Make a back-up copy of your work

When revising/editing:

1. Complete printout
2. General revision of whole document or in chunks
3. Input changes, and do another printout
4. Revise/edit, input changes and give yourself a new printout

   until satisfied

Spell check ...

- Won't pick up everything
- Won't check your punctuation

Grammar check ...

If grammar's not your strong point, this may help.

TIPS ON WORD PROCESSING

"Always make a backup copy of your work."

In revising and editing, some of us edit directly on screen. I prefer to give myself a printout from which to work. In my experience, this is a good way to proceed:

1. Once you've written your draft, give yourself a printout.

2. Read it, then revise/edit the printout. Here's where wide margins and double/triple spacing really help. Not only do I rewrite but there are arrows all over the place where I want something inserted, or sentences and paragraphs put in a different place.

3. You can revise/edit the whole printout, or, do it in sections, or chunks (See the section above.) If it's short, like a letter, do it in one pass. If there are several sections, I often revise/edit each section on its own – which makes the revisions extremely manageable.

4. Input changes, give yourself another printout, read and revise as necessary until you're satisfied that your work is complete.

Spell check on your computer

Spell check helps proof your spelling. However it won't pick up the error if you've typed *the* where you meant to say *they*. Reading out loud will do that.

Spell check won't detect your use of *whose* instead of *who's* either. For this kind of error and for mistakes in punctuation, you'll need to examine your text more closely.

Grammar check on your computer

As well as programs that are built into software like MS Word, other excellent grammar checkers are available. Make use of them. They're very helpful in sentence construction, especially for tricky areas such as when to use colons and semi-colons.

Like spell check, however, grammar checkers won't necessarily catch or correct all of your grammatical errors. That's where reading out loud can help. 155

*One last look may
lead to a significant
improvement in your
presentation*

take one last look

The more I talk with instructors, writers, communicators and students, the more they agree that wherever possible, it's smart to set your work aside for a couple of days before taking one last look at what you've created.

The reasoning is that you've been so close to your work during the writing process, that there's been no break to review what you've written with fresh eyes.

When you take that one last look, you may be sufficiently satisfied and change nothing. On the other hand, you may find that you wish to improve something you've written, provide fresh evidence to bolster an argument, or add further input that you believe would make a difference to your presentation.

This one last look is to satisfy yourself that you've done your best. It is not about perfection. I know that I can nitpick an assignment to death, changing a word here, a phrase there, without really making a difference to the overall result. So avoid *over editing*.

When you know you've done your best, let the assignment stand on its own and be judged on its merits.

APA. *Publication Manual of the American Psychological Association*. 6th ed. Washington: American Psychological Association, 2009. Print.

APA. *APA Style*. American Psychological Association. 2011. Web. <http://www.apastyle.org>.

Buzan, Tony. *Use Your Head*. Upper Saddle River, NJ: Pearson Education, 2010. Print.

Buzan, Tony and Barry Buzan. *The Mind Map Book*. Ed. James Harrison. Upper Saddle River, NJ: FT Press, 2010. Print.

Covey, Stephen, R. *The 7 Habits of Highly Effective People*. Rev. ed. New York: Free Press, 2004. Print.

Fogarty, Mignon. *Grammar Girl's Quick and Dirty Tips for Better Writing*. New York: Holt Paperbacks, 2008. Print.

Goldberg, Natalie. *Writing Down the Bones*. Exp. ed. Boston: Shambhala, 2010. Print

Hacker, Diana. *A Writer's Reference*. 6th ed. Boston: Bedford Books of St. Martin's Press, 2010. Print.

Klauser, Henriette Anne. *Writing on Both Sides of the Brain*. San Francisco: HarperOne, 1987. Print.

MLA. MLA *Handbook for Writers of Research Papers*. 7th ed. New York: The Modern Language Association of America, 2009. Print.

MLA. *MLA Style*. The Modern Language Association of America. 2011. Web. <http://www.mla.org>.

Rico, Gabriele. *Writing the Natural Way*. Rev. Sub. ed. New York: Tarcher, 2000. Print.

Strunk Jr., William and E.B. White. *The Elements of Style*. 50th Anv. ed. White Plains, NY: Longman, 2008. Print.

Truss, Lynne. *Eats, Shoots & Leaves*. New York: Gotham, 2006. Print.

The following resources have been invaluable to me:

The work of Tony Buzan.
You can find more information on books, tapes and seminars by Tony Buzan at http://www.thinkbuzan.com

The skills of Phil Chambers.
Phil is an expert on the use of mind mapping.
Phil's website is: www.learning-tech.co.uk

The expertise of Extraordinary Conversations.
Extraordinary Conversations! is a Toronto-based management consulting firm specializing in cultural transformation, leadership development and organizational renewal. For more information on presentations, tapes and seminars in these areas, including listening and speaking, contact:

Extraordinary Conversations Inc.
20 Dacre Crescent
Toronto, ON, M6S 2W1
Tel: (416) 361-3331 Fax: (416) 361-3284
Email: lynne@extraordinaryconversations.com
www.extraordinaryconversations.com

ALSO BY NEIL SAWERS

"A superb, easy-to-use guidebook recommended for business writers of all skill and experience levels."
– The Midwest Book Review
The Business Shelf

ISBN: 978-0-9697901-4-3

$16.95

www.how-to-write-proposals.com